D0372339

WAR AT HOME

Covert Action Against U.S. Activists and What We Can Do About It

Brian Glick

SOUTH END PRESS

Boston, MA

No. 6 in the South End Press Pamphlet Series

Acknowledgements: Special thanks to Kim Christensen and Mike Spiegel for their profound contribution to the politics and presentation of this book. Thanks also to Paul Acinapura, Rafael Anglada López, Linda Backiel, Jill Benderly, Chip Berlet, Peter Bohmer, Kathy Boudin, Ann Mari Buitrago, Haywood Burns, Seymour Cabin, Fritz Capria, Ward Churchill, Mona Clarke, Kathleen Cleaver, Matthew Countryman, Peter Countryman, Hillary Exter, Larry Goldfarb, Jill Hamberg, Ellen Herman, Todd Jailer, Jeff Jones, Muhammed Kenyatta, Sylvia Law, Ken Lawrence, Linda Lotz, Jesse Mentkhen, Ron Milcarek, Sue Novick, the People's Law Office (Chicago), John Roberts, Kathy Roberts, Emma Sabin, Jeff Segal, Eleanor Stein, Dan Stern, Bill Strickland, and Leonard Weinglass.

Publication of this pamphlet assisted by a grant from the Civil Liberties Committee of the National Lawyers Guild. ⚖

first edition
cover by Mike Spiegel and Loie Hayes
design and production by the South End Press collective
manufactured in the U.S.A.

Library of Congress Cataloging-in-Publication Data
Glick, Brian.
    War at home.
    (South End Press pamphlet series ; no. 6)
    Bibliography: p.
    1. United States. Federal Bureau of Investigation.
2. Political persecution--United States. 3. United
States--Politics and government--1981- . I. Title.
HV8141.G57 1988   353.0074   88-30840
ISBN 0-89608-349-7

South End Press, 116 Saint Botolph St., Boston, MA 02115
  2 3 4 5 6 7 8 9   97 96 95 94 93 92 91 90 89

CONTENTS

Introduction

In January 1988, the people of the United States learned of a secret nationwide FBI campaign against the domestic opponents of U.S. policy in Central America. Government documents obtained through the Freedom of Information Act show that from 1981 through at least 1985, the FBI infiltrated the Committee in Solidarity with the People of El Salvador (CISPES) and disrupted its work all across the country. The investigation eventually reached into nearly every sector of the anti-intervention movement, from the Maryknoll Sisters, the Southern Christian Leadership Conference, and the New Jewish Agenda to the United Auto Workers, the United Steel Workers, U.S. Senator Christopher Dodd, and U.S. Representatives Pat Schroeder and Jim Wright.[1]

Some of the goals and methods of this campaign were revealed by a central participant, Frank Varelli. Varelli admitted that from 1981 through 1984, the FBI paid him to infiltrate and "break" the Dallas, Texas chapter of CISPES. To this end, he and his cohorts put out bogus literature under the CISPES name, burglarized CISPES members' homes, and paid right-wing students to start fights at CISPES rallies. Varelli was told to seduce an activist nun to get blackmail photos for the FBI. It was also suggested that he plant guns on CISPES members. As part of his work, he routinely exchanged information about U.S. and Central American activists with the Salvadoran National Guard, sponsor of that country's death squads.[2]

Elsewhere in the Southwest, in 1984, government informers surfaced as the main witnesses in the federal prosecution of clergy and lay workers providing sanctuary for refugees from El Salvador and Guatemala. Salomón Graham and Jesús Cruz testified that they were paid by the U.S. Immigration and Naturalization Service (INS) to infiltrate church services, Bible classes, and sanctuary support networks. They were part of "Operation Sojourner," the U.S. Justice Department's countrywide crackdown on sanctuary churches and organizations.[3]

In the San Francisco Bay Area, in the early 1980s, the Livermore Action Group's meetings to plan anti-nuclear civil disobedience were similarly infiltrated by both the U.S. Navy and the Federal Emergency Management Administration.[4] The FBI has admitted such operations from 1982-84 against the Bay Area branches of Physicians for Social

1

Responsibility and other peace groups.[5] In September 1987, the Bureau fired Special Agent John Ryan for refusing to conduct a similar "terrorism investigation" of the Illinois peace group, Veterans Fast for Life.[6]

In Albany, New York in 1981, the FBI and police infiltrated and disrupted the Capital District Coalition Against Apartheid and Racism (CDCAAR). At 3 a.m. on the day of the group's protest against the U.S. tour of the South African Springbok rugby team, FBI agents and state and local police broke into the home of CDCAAR leader Vera Michelson. Supposedly acting on an anonymous FBI informer's false report that the anti-apartheid activists were stockpiling weapons, the officers burst into Michelson's bedroom, put a shotgun to her head, and forced her to crawl to another part of the apartment where she was handcuffed to a table. They then ransacked the apartment, confiscating CDCAAR files along with private papers and address books. Michelson and two other organizers were detained on bogus charges and kept from participating in the demonstration. They later learned that the same FBI infiltrator had spread false reports of planned violence in order to discourage participation in the demonstration.[7]

Other forms of government harassment hit activists who spent time in Nicaragua or Cuba during the 1980s. Travelers and travel agencies were audited by the Internal Revenue Service. Private papers were copied or confiscated at the border. Mail arrived late and open, or never arrived. Returnees' homes, jobs, churches, and communities were hounded by the FBI.[8] World-renowned feminist author Margaret Randall, a former U.S. citizen who returned home after several years in Cuba and Nicaragua, was denied permanent residence status and ordered to leave the United States solely on the basis of the political content of her writings.[9]

Churches and organizations opposed to U.S. policy in Central America reported more than 300 incidents of harassment from 1984 through 1988, including nearly 100 break-ins. Important papers, files, and computer disks were stolen or found damaged and strewn about, while money and valuables were left untouched. License plates on a car seen fleeing an attempted burglary of the Washington, D.C. office of Sojourners, a religious group that helped form the Pledge of Resistance to U.S. war in Central America, were traced to the U.S. National Security Agency. Other incidents were also attributed to government agents or to "private" right-wing groups backed by Lt. Col. Oliver North at the National Security Council. The FBI repeatedly rejected congressional calls for a federal probe.[10]

Similar break-ins were experienced throughout 1987-88 by U.S. supporters of Palestinian self-determination. On January 26, 1988, the

There's this lady statue holding a torch who's supposed to welcome the tired and poor looking for freedom.

But she doesn't seem as glad to see some of us as others.

She's not crazy about folks who don't speak English and aren't white and don't have much education.

She really can't stand folks from certain countries that the U.S. government tells her not to like.

So a little advice for all you huddled masses:

Ditch the lady with the torch and come in over the Mexican border.

© anlesquith 2/2/87

FBI, INS, and Los Angeles police arrested eight activists for deportation as "terrorists." The evidence against them consisted solely of photos showing that they helped distribute magazines published by the Popular Front for the Liberation of Palestine. As the eight appealed the INS ruling, their homes were burglarized and boxes of files on their case were stolen from the cars of American Friends Service Committee staff and others active in their defense. Secret INS plans uncovered in February 1988 call for thousands more U.S. Arab-American activists to be rounded up and deported as "alien terrorists and undesirables."[11]

The same terrorist label provided the pretext for recent FBI attacks on the movement for Puerto Rico's independence from U.S. colonial rule. On August 30, 1985, hundreds of FBI agents, backed by military helicopters, rounded up prominent independentistas and charged them with being members of Los Macheteros, a clandestine independence organization. The raiders destroyed the editorial offices and printing presses of the progressive journal *Pensamiento Crítico* and ransacked the homes and offices of 38 well-known poets, artists, trade unionists, labor lawyers, and community organizers. Thirteen were held incommunicado for days and publicly branded as "terrorists." Finally charged with conspiracy to rob a Wells Fargo depot in Hartford, Connecticut, nine were kept in U.S. jails for more than a year, two for nearly three years, under new federal preventive detention laws. One of those two, Filiberto Ojeda Rios, who is 55 years old and has a serious heart condition, was released under court order in May 1988 but quickly re-jailed (for having defended himself and resisted arrest during the 1985 raid) and again held without bail. Although the defendants are Spanish speaking, the court acceded to the prosecution's demand that they be tried in English, more than 1000 miles from their families and homeland. Pre-trial hearings implicated the FBI in falsified reports, alteration of evidence, burglaries, illegal surveillance, and intimidation of witnesses.[12]

A comparable show of paramilitary might accompanied the October 18, 1984 arrest of eight New York City Black activists. A "Joint Anti-Terrorist Task Force" of more than 500 FBI and police agents, wielding machine guns and a bazooka, cordoned off entire city blocks to arrest law school graduates, city housing managers, college students, and a union steward. Promising community projects were disrupted while the eight were held for weeks without bail and placed for almost a year under strict curfew, while their co-workers were jailed for refusing to testify before a grand jury. Acquitted of the major charges when jurors rejected the claims of a police infiltrator, the eight faced continued police harassment. One was later framed on bogus weapons charges, along with two other leaders of a Brooklyn community group, Black Men Against Crack.[13]

In Alabama, in the mid-1980s, the FBI mounted an even more massive effort to intimidate grassroots supporters of Jesse Jackson's presidential campaign and to crush the emerging pro-Jackson Black leadership based in the Campaign for a New South.

Immediately after the September 1984 primaries in Alabama, as many as two hundred FBI agents swept through the five western Alabama Black Belt counties that had given their votes to Jesse Jackson, rousing elderly people from their beds in the middle of the night, taking about one thousand of them in police-escorted buses to Mobile to be finger-printed, and suggesting that their absentee ballots may have been tampered with by the civil rights workers who had secured their votes. The offices of civil rights workers were also raided and some of the documents they needed for the November elections were confiscated.

In January 1985, indictments for vote and mail fraud were handed down against eight of the Black Belt's most experienced organizers and political leaders. In bringing the indictments, the federal government used the Voting Rights Act of 1965, the very act most of these people had marched from Selma to Montgomery to get enacted.[14]

Although the defendants were acquitted of all major charges and their organization survived, the raids, interrogations, arrests, and trials took a heavy toll.

***

Government harassment of U.S. political activists clearly exists today, violating our fundamental democratic rights and creating a climate of fear and distrust which undermines our efforts to challenge official policy. Similar attacks on social justice movements came to light during the 1960s. Only years later did we learn that these had been merely the visible tip of an iceberg. Largely hidden at the time was a vast government program to neutralize domestic political opposition through "covert action" (political repression carried out secretly or under the guise of legitimate law enforcement).

The 1960s program, coordinated by the FBI under the code name "COINTELPRO," was exposed in the 1970s and supposedly stopped. But covert operations against domestic dissidents did not end. They have persisted and become an integral part of government activity. This book is designed to help today's activists learn from the history of COINTELPRO, so that future movements can better fight this war at home.

The opening section reviews what we know about COINTELPRO. It explains how the program was uncovered when the FBI and police were compelled to release previously secret documents. It outlines COINTELPRO's methods and targets and assesses its contribution to the decline of the movements of the 1960s.

The next section shows that domestic covert action did not end when COINTELPRO was officially disbanded. It remained in effect under other names and it continues to be a serious threat today. Persisting under Democratic as well as Republican administrations, it has become a permanent feature of U.S. politics.

The final section discusses what we can do about this danger. It analyzes the specific methods used in COINTELPRO—infiltration, psychological warfare, harassment through the legal system, and extralegal force and violence—and proposes steps to limit or deflect their impact on our movements. It shows that these methods do not protect "national security" or combat terrorism, as claimed by the government, but actually serve to foment violence and subvert democracy. Various tactics are suggested for publicly exposing the reality of domestic covert action and mobilizing broad-based protest against its continued use.

Excerpts from key COINTELPRO documents are reproduced at the back of the book, along with a list of resource groups and additional readings.

Domestic covert action is a powerful deterrent to democratic discussion of public policy and effective organizing for social change. We need to take it seriously without being distracted from our main goals. Please talk with other activists about the analysis and recommendations presented here. Adapt the guidelines to the conditions you face. Point out problems and suggest other approaches.

Now is the time to begin fighting the hidden war at home.

COINTELPRO: Covert Action Against the Domestic Dissidents of the 1960s

While much FBI and police harassment was blatant during the 1960s, and surveillance and infiltration were suspected, talk of CIA-style covert action against domestic dissidents was generally dismissed as "paranoia." It was not until the 1970s, after the damage had been done, that the sordid history of COINTELPRO began to emerge. This Chapter describes how COINTELPRO was uncovered and what we now know of its methods, targets, and impact.

• How We Learned About COINTELPRO

The first concrete evidence of COINTELPRO surfaced in March 1971, when a "Citizens Committee to Investigate the FBI" removed secret files from an FBI office in Media, Pennsylvania and released them to the press.[15] That same year, agents began to resign from the Bureau and to blow the whistle on its covert operations.[16] These revelations came at a time of enormous social unrest and declining public confidence in government. Publication of the *Pentagon Papers* in September 1971 exposed years of systematic official lies about the Vietnam War. Soon it was learned that a clandestine squad of White House "plumbers" had broken into Daniel Ellsberg's psychiatrist's office in an effort to smear the former Pentagon staffer who had leaked the top-secret papers to the press.[17]

The same "plumbers" were caught the following year burglarizing the Watergate offices of the Democratic National Committee. Nationally televised congressional hearings on Watergate revealed a full-blown program of "dirty tricks" to subvert the anti-war movement as well as the

Democratic Party by forging letters, leaking false news items to the press, stealing files, and roughing up demonstrators. Lines of command for these operations were traced to Attorney General Mitchell and the White House, with the FBI implicated in a massive cover-up involving President Nixon and his top staff. By 1971, congressional hearings had already disclosed U.S. Army infiltration of domestic political movements. Similar CIA and local police activity soon came to light, along with ghastly accounts of CIA operations abroad to destabilize democratically elected governments and assassinate heads of state.

This crisis was eventually resolved through what historian Howard Zinn describes as "a complex process of consolidation," based on "the need to satisfy a disillusioned public that the system was criticizing and correcting itself."[18] In this process, the U.S. Freedom of Information Act (FOIA) was amended over President Nixon's veto to provide some degree of genuine public access to FBI documents. Lawsuits under the FOIA forced the Bureau to release some COINTELPRO files to major news media. By 1975, both houses of Congress had launched formal inquiries into government "intelligence activities."

The agencies under congressional investigation were allowed to withhold most of their files and to edit the Senate Committee's reports before publication.[19] The House Committee's report, including an account of FBI and CIA obstruction of its inquiry, was suppressed altogether after part was leaked to the press.[20] Still, pressure to promote the appearance of genuine reform was so great that the FBI had to divulge an unprecedented, detailed account of many of its domestic covert operations.

Many important files continue to be withheld, and others have been destroyed.[21] Former operatives report that the most heinous and embarrassing actions were never committed to writing.[22] Officials with

We're from the federal Bureau of Investigation.   Why me?   We've been watching you. You dress funny. You go to meetings.   But it's a free country.

broad personal knowledge of COINTELPRO have been silenced, most notably William C. Sullivan, who created the program and ran it throughout the 1960s. Sullivan was killed in an uninvestigated 1977 "hunting accident" shortly after giving extensive information to a grand jury investigating the FBI, but before he could testify publicly.[23] Nevertheless, a great deal has been learned about COINTELPRO.

• How COINTELPRO Worked

When congressional investigations, political trials, and other traditional legal modes of repression failed to counter the growing movements, and even helped to fuel them, the FBI and police moved outside the law. They resorted to the secret and systematic use of fraud and force to sabotage constitutionally protected political activity. Their methods ranged far beyond surveillance, amounting to a homefront version of the covert action for which the CIA has become infamous throughout the world.

FBI Headquarters secretly instructed its field offices to propose schemes to "expose, disrupt, misdirect, discredit, or otherwise neutralize" specific individuals and groups.[24] Close coordination with local police and prosecutors was strongly encouraged. Other recommended collaborators included friendly news media, business and foundation executives, and university, church, and trade union officials, as well as such "patriotic" organizations as the American Legion.

Final authority rested with FBI Headquarters in Washington, D.C. Top FBI officials pressed local field offices to step up their activity and demanded regular progress reports. Agents were directed to maintain full secrecy "such that under no circumstances should the existence of the program be made known outside the Bureau and appropriate

within-office security should be afforded to sensitive operations and techniques."[25] A total of 2,370 officially approved COINTELPRO actions were admitted to the Senate Intelligence Committee,[26] and thousands more have since been uncovered.

Four main methods have been revealed:

1. **Infiltration:** Agents and informers did not merely spy on political activists. Their main purpose was to discredit and disrupt. Their very presence served to undermine trust and scare off potential supporters. The FBI and police exploited this fear to smear genuine activists as agents.

2. **Psychological Warfare From the Outside:** The FBI and police used myriad other "dirty tricks" to undermine progressive movements. They planted false media stories and published bogus leaflets and other publications in the name of targeted groups. They forged correspondence, sent anonymous letters, and made anonymous telephone calls. They spread misinformation about meetings and events, set up pseudo movement groups run by government agents, and manipulated or strong-armed parents, employers, landlords, school officials and others to cause trouble for activists.

3. **Harassment Through the Legal System:** The FBI and police abused the legal system to harass dissidents and make them appear to be criminals. Officers of the law gave perjured testimony and presented fabricated evidence as a pretext for false arrests and wrongful imprisonment. They discriminatorily enforced tax laws and other government regulations and used conspicuous surveillance, "investigative" interviews, and grand jury subpoenas in an effort to intimidate activists and silence their supporters.

4. **Extralegal Force and Violence:** The FBI and police threatened, instigated, and themselves conducted break-ins, vandalism, assaults, and beatings. The object was to frighten dissidents and disrupt their movements. In the case of radical Black and Puerto Rican activists (and later Native Americans), these attacks—including political assassinations—were so extensive, vicious, and calculated that they can accurately be termed a form of official "terrorism."

Each of these COINTELPRO methods is described and analyzed in detail on pages 41-65. Specific examples from the documentary record of the 1960s are presented there, along with practical suggestions for coping with similar attacks in the future.

• COINTELPRO's Main Targets

Though the name COINTELPRO stands for "Counterintelligence Program," the government's targets were not enemy spies. The Senate

Intelligence Committee later found that "Under COINTELPRO certain techniques the Bureau had used against hostile foreign agents were adopted for use against perceived domestic threats to the established political and social order."[27]

The most intense COINTELPRO operations were directed against the Black movement, particularly the Black Panther Party. This was to some extent a function of the racism of the FBI and police, as well as the vulnerability of the Black community (due to its lack of ties to political and economic elites and the tendency of the media—and whites in general—to ignore or tolerate attacks on Black groups). At a deeper level, the choice of targets reflects government and corporate fear of a militant, broad-based Black movement. Such a movement is dangerous because of its historic capacity to galvanize widespread rebellion at home and its repercussions for the U.S. image abroad. Moreover, Black people's location in major urban centers and primary industries gives them the potential to disrupt the base of the U.S. economy.

COINTELPRO's targets were not, however, limited to Black militants. Many other activists who wanted to end U.S. intervention abroad or institute racial, gender, and class justice at home also came under attack. César Chávez, Fathers Daniel and Phillip Berrigan, Rev. Jesse Jackson, David Dellinger, officials of the American Friends Service Committee and the National Council of Churches, and other leading pacifists were high on the list, as were projects directly protected by the First Amendment, such as anti-war teach-ins, progressive bookstores, independent filmmakers, and alternative newspapers and news services.[28] Martin Luther King, Jr., world-renowned prophet of nonviolence, was the object of sustained FBI assault. King was marked, barely a month before his murder, for elimination as a potential "messiah" who could "unify and electrify" the Black movement.[29]

Ultimately, FBI documents disclosed six major official counterintelligence programs (as well as non-COINTELPRO covert operations against Native American, Asian-American, Arab-American, Iranian, and other activists):

"Communist Party-USA" (1956-71): This was the first and largest program, which contributed to the Party's decline in the late 1950s and was used in the early and mid-1960s mainly against civil rights, civil liberties, and peace activists. Its targets during the latter period included Martin Luther King, Jr., the Mississippi Freedom Democratic Party, the NAACP, the National Lawyers Guild, the National Committee to Abolish the House Un-American Activities Committee, Women's Strike for Peace, the American Friends Service Committee, and the National Committee for a SANE Nuclear Policy.

"Groups Seeking Independence for Puerto Rico" (1960-71): Initially hidden from congressional investigators, and still one of the least well known, this program functioned to disrupt, discredit, and faction-alize the island's main centers of anti-colonial resistance, especially the Puerto Rican Socialist Party (PSP) and Socialist League (LSP). It also appears to have targeted groups fighting for human rights for Puerto Ricans living in the United States, such as the Young Lords Party.

"Border Coverage Program" (1960-71): This program of covert operations against radical Mexican organizations was similarly con-cealed from Congress. The few documents released to date do not indicate how much the FBI used it against 1960s Chicano activists such as the Brown Berets, the Crusade for Justice (Colorado), La Alianza (New Mexico), and the Chicano Moratorium to End the War in Vietnam (Los Angeles), which are known to have been infiltrated and repressed by other government agencies.

"Socialist Workers Party" (1961-69): In addition to ongoing attacks on the SWP and its youth group, the Young Socialist Alliance, this program operated against whomever those groups supported or worked with, especially Malcolm X and the National Mobilization Com-mittee to End the War in Vietnam.

"Black Nationalist Hate Groups" (1967-71): This was the vehicle for the Bureau's all-out assault on Martin Luther King, Jr. (in the late 1960s), the Student Non-Violent Coordinating Committee (SNCC), the Congress of Racial Equality (CORE), the Black Panther Party, the Nation of Islam ("Black Muslims"), the National Welfare Rights Organization, the League of Black Revolutionary Workers, the Dodge Revolutionary Union Movement (DRUM), the Revolutionary Action Movement (RAM), the Republic of New Afrika (RNA), the Congress of African People, Black student unions, and many local Black churches and community or-ganizations struggling for decent living conditions, justice, equality, and empowerment.

"New Left" (1968-71): A program to destroy Students for a Democratic Society (SDS), the Peace and Freedom Party, the Institute for Policy Studies, and a broad range of anti-war, anti-racist, student, GI, veteran, feminist, lesbian, gay, environmental, Marxist, and anarchist groups, as well as the network of food co-ops, health clinics, child care centers, schools, bookstores, newspapers, community centers, street theaters, rock groups, and communes that formed the infrastructure of the counter-culture.

"White Hate Groups" (1964-71): This unique "program" func-tioned largely as a component of the FBI's operations against the progres-sive activists who were COINTELPRO's main targets. Under the cover of being even-handed and going after violent right-wing groups, the FBI actually gave covert aid to the Ku Klux Klan, Minutemen, Nazis, and other racist vigilantes. These groups received substantial funds, information, and protection—and suffered only token FBI harassment—so long as they directed their violence against COINTELPRO targets. They were not subjected to serious disruption unless they breached this tacit understanding and attacked established business and political leaders.

• How COINTELPRO Helped Destroy the Movements of the 1960s[30]

Since COINTELPRO was used mainly against the progressive movements of the 1960s, its impact can be grasped only in the context of the momentous social upheaval which shook the country during those years.

All across the United States, Black communities came alive with renewed political struggle. Most major cities experienced sustained, disciplined Black protest and massive ghetto uprisings. Black activists galvanized multi-racial rebellion among GIs, welfare mothers, students, and prisoners.

College campuses and high schools erupted in militant protest against the Vietnam War. A predominantly white New Left, inspired by the Black movement, fought for an end to U.S. intervention abroad and a more humane and cooperative way of life at home. By the late 1960s, deep-rooted resistance had revived among Chicanos, Puerto Ricans, Asian Americans, and Native Americans. A second wave of broad-based struggle for women's liberation had also emerged, along with significant efforts by lesbians, gay men, and disabled people.

Millions of people in the United States began to reject the dominant ideology and culture. Thousands challenged basic U.S. political and economic institutions. For a brief moment, "the crucial mixture of people's confidence in the government and lack of confidence in themselves which allows the government to govern, the ruling class to rule...threatened to break down."[31]

By the mid-1970s, this upheaval had largely subsided. Important progressive activity persisted, mainly on a local level, and much continued to be learned and won, but the massive, militant Black and New Left movements were gone. The sense of infinite possibility and of our collective power to shape the future had been lost. Progressive momentum dissipated. Radicals found themselves on the defensive as right-wing extremists gained major government positions and defined the contours of accepted political debate.

Many factors besides COINTELPRO contributed to this change. Important progress was made toward achieving movement goals such as Black civil rights, an end to the Vietnam War, and university reform. The mass media, owned by big business and cowed by government and right-wing attack, helped to bury radical activism by ceasing to cover it. Television, popular magazines, and daily papers stereotyped Blacks as hardened criminals and welfare chiselers or as the supposedly affluent beneficiaries of reverse "discrimination." White youth were portrayed first as hedonistic hippies and mindless terrorists, later as an apolitical, self-indulgent "me generation." Both were scapegoated as threats to "decent, hard-working Middle America."

During the severe economic recession of the early- to mid- 1970s, former student activists began entering the job market, some taking on responsibility for children. Many were scared by brutal government and right-wing attacks culminating in the murder of rank-and-file activists as well as prominent leaders. Some were strung out on the hard drugs that had become increasingly available in Black and Latin communities and among white youth. Others were disillusioned by mistreatment in movements ravaged by the very social sicknesses they sought to eradicate, including racism, sexism, homophobia, class bias and competition.

Limited by their upbringing, social position, and isolation from older radical traditions, 1960s activists were unable to make the connections and changes required to build movements strong enough to survive and eventually win structural change in the United States. Middle-class students did not sufficiently ally with working and poor people. Too few white activists accepted third world leadership of multi-racial alliances. Too many men refused to practice genuine gender equality.

Originally motivated by goals of quick reforms, 1960s activists were ill-prepared for the long-term struggles in which they found themselves. Overly dependent on media-oriented superstars and one-shot dramatic actions, they failed to develop stable organizations, accountable leadership, and strategic perspective. Creatures of the culture they so despised, they often lacked the patience to sustain tedious grassroots work and painstaking analysis of actual social conditions. They found it hard to accept the slow, uneven pace of personal and political change.

This combination of circumstances, however, did not by itself guarantee political collapse. The achievements of the 1960s movements could have inspired optimism and provided a sense of the power to win other important struggles. The rightward shift of the major media could have enabled alternative newspapers, magazines, theater, film, and video to attract a broader audience and stable funding. The economic downturn of the early 1970s could have united Black militants, New

Leftists, and workers in common struggle. Police brutality and government collusion in drug trafficking could have been exposed in ways that undermined support for the authorities and broadened the movements' backing.

By the close of the decade, many of the movements' internal weaknesses were starting to be addressed. Black-led multi-racial alliances, such as Martin Luther King, Jr.'s Poor People's Campaign and the Black Panthers' Rainbow Coalition, were forming. The movements' class base was broadening through Black "revolutionary unions" in auto and other industries, King's increasing focus on economic issues, the New Left's spread to community colleges, and the return of working-class GIs radicalized by their experience in Vietnam. At the same time, the women's movement was confronting the deep sexism which permeated 1960s activism, along with its corollaries: homophobia, sexual violence, militarism, competitiveness, and top-down decision-making.

While the problems of the 1960s movements were enormous, their strengths might have enabled them to overcome their weaknesses had the upsurge not been stifled before activists could learn from their mistakes. Much of the movements' inability to transcend their initial limitations and overcome adversity can be traced to COINTELPRO.

It was through COINTELPRO that the public image of Blacks and New Leftists was distorted to legitimize their arrest and imprisonment and scapegoat them as the cause of working people's problems. The FBI and police instigated violence and fabricated movement horrors. Dissidents were deliberately "criminalized" through false charges, frame-ups, and offensive, bogus leaflets and other materials published in their name. (Specific examples of these and other COINTELPRO operations are presented on pages 41-65.)

COINTELPRO enabled the FBI and police to exacerbate the movements' internal stresses until beleaguered activists turned on one another. Whites were pitted against Blacks, Blacks against Chicanos and Puerto Ricans, students against workers, workers against people on welfare, men against women, religious activists against atheists, Christians against Jews, Jews against Muslims. "Anonymous" accusations of infidelity ripped couples apart. Backers of women's and gay liberation were attacked as "dykes" or "faggots." Money was repeatedly stolen and precious equipment sabotaged to intensify pressure and sow suspicion and mistrust.

Otherwise manageable disagreements were inflamed by COINTELPRO until they erupted into hostile splits that shattered alliances, tore groups apart, and drove dedicated activists out of the movement. Government documents implicate the FBI and police in the bitter break-up of such pivotal groups as the Black Panther Party, SDS, and the Liberation News Service, and in the collapse of repeated efforts to form long-term coalitions across racial, class, and regional lines. While genuine political issues were often involved in these disputes, the outcome could have been different if government agencies had not covertly intervened to subvert compromise and fuel hostility and competition.

Finally, it was COINTELPRO that enabled the FBI and police to eliminate the leaders of mass movements without undermining the image of the United States as a democracy, complete with free speech and the rule of law. Charismatic orators and dynamic organizers were covertly attacked and "neutralized" before their skills could be transferred to others and stable structures established to carry on their work. Malcolm X was killed in a "factional dispute" which the FBI took credit for having "developed" in the Nation of Islam.[32] Martin Luther King, Jr. was the target of an elaborate FBI plot to drive him to suicide and replace him "in his role of the leadership of the Negro people" with conservative Black lawyer Samuel Pierce (later named to Reagan's cabinet).[33] Many have come to view King's eventual assassination (and Malcolm's as well) as itself a domestic covert operation.[34]

Other prominent radicals faced similar attack when they began to develop broad followings and express anti-capitalist ideas. Some were portrayed as crooks, thugs, philanderers, or government agents, while others were physically threatened or assaulted until they abandoned their work. Still others were murdered under phony pretexts, such as "shootouts" in which the only shots were fired by the police.

To help bring down a major target, the FBI often combined these approaches in strategic sequence. Take the case of the "underground press," a network of some 400 radical weeklies and several national news services, which once boasted a combined readership of close to 30 million. In the late 1960s, government agents raided the offices of alternative newspapers across the country in purported pursuit of drugs and fugitives. In the process, they destroyed typewriters, cameras, printing presses, layout equipment, business records, and research files, and roughed up and jailed staffers on bogus charges. Meanwhile, the FBI was persuading record companies to withdraw lucrative advertising and arranging for printers, suppliers, and distributors to drop underground press accounts. With their already shaky operations in disarray, the papers and news services were easy targets for a final phase of COINTELPRO disruption. Forged correspondence, anonymous accusations, and infiltrators' manipulation provoked a flurry of wild charges and

This is a free
country.

March in the
Streets.

Publish your
radical newspapers.

Boycott grapes
every now and
again.

But if you think
for one minute that
we're actually going to
let you make any
real change ...

You're more
outa your
minds than
we thought.

© abesmich 1/87

counter-charges that played a major role in bringing many of these promising endeavors to a premature end.[35]

A similar pattern can be discerned from the history of the Black Panther Party. Brutal government attacks initially elicited broad support for this new, militant, highly visible national organization and its popular ten-point socialist program for Black self-determination. But the FBI's repressive onslaught severely weakened the Party, making it vulnerable to sophisticated FBI psychological warfare which so discredited and shattered it that few people today have any notion of the power and potential that the Panthers once represented.[36]

What proved most devastating in all of this was the effective manipulation of the victims of COINTELPRO into blaming themselves. Since the FBI and police operated covertly, the horrors they engineered appeared to emanate from within the movements. Activists' trust in one another and in their collective power was subverted, and the hopes of a generation died, leaving a legacy of cynicism and despair which continues to haunt us today.

Black Panther Party Program: What We Want
— adopted 1966

1. We want freedom. We want power to determine the destiny of our Black Community.

2. We want full employment for our people.

3. We want an end to the robbery by the CAPITALIST of our Black Community.

4. We want decent housing, fit for shelter of human beings.

5. We want education for our people that exposes the true nature of this decadent American society. We want education that teaches us our true history and our role in the present-day society.

6. We want all black men to be exempt from military service.

7. We want an immediate end to POLICE BRUTALITY and MURDER of black people.

8. We want freedom for all black men held in federal, state, county and city prisons and jails.

9. We want all black people when brought to trial to be tried in court by a jury of their peer group or people from their black communities, as defined by the Constitution of the United States.

10. We want land, bread, housing, education, clothing, justice and peace. And as our major political objective, a United Nations-supervised plebiscite to be held throughout the black colony in which only black colonial subjects will be allowed to participate, for the purpose of determining the will of black people as to their national destiny.

Domestic Covert Action Remains a Serious Threat Today

The public exposure of COINTELPRO and other government abuses elicited a flurry of apparent reform in the 1970s. President Nixon resigned in the face of impeachment. His Attorney General, other top aides, and many of the "plumbers" were prosecuted and imprisoned for brief periods. The CIA's director and counter-intelligence chief were ousted, and the CIA and the Army were again directed to cease covert operations against domestic targets.[37]

The FBI had formally shut down COINTELPRO a few weeks after it was uncovered. As part of the general face-lift, the Bureau publicly apologized for COINTELPRO, and municipal governments began to disband the local police "red squads" that had served as the FBI's main accomplices. A new Attorney General notified several hundred activists that they had been victims of COINTELPRO and issued guidelines limiting future operations. Top FBI officials were indicted for ordering the burglary of activists' offices and homes; two were convicted, and several others retired or resigned. The Bureau's egomaniacal, crudely racist and sexist founder, J. Edgar Hoover, died in 1972. After two interim directors failed to stem the tide of criticism, a prestigious federal judge, William Webster, was appointed by President Carter to clean house and build a "new FBI."[38]

Behind this public hoopla, however, the Bureau's war at home continued unabated. Domestic covert action did not end when it was exposed in the 1970s. It has persisted throughout the 1980s and become a permanent feature of U.S. government.

• Domestic Covert Action Did Not End in the 1970s

Director Webster's highly touted reforms did not create a "new FBI." They served mainly to modernize the existing Bureau and to make it even more dangerous. In place of the backbiting competition with other law enforcement and intelligence agencies which had previously impeded coordination of domestic counter-insurgency, Webster promoted inter-agency cooperation. Adopting the mantle of an "equal opportunity employer," his FBI hired women and people of color to more effectively penetrate a broader range of political targets. By cultivating a low-visibility image and discreetly avoiding public attack on prominent liberals, Webster gradually restored the Bureau's respectability and won over a number of its former critics.[39]

State and local police similarly upgraded their repressive capabilities in the 1970s while learning to present a more friendly public face. The "red squads" that had harassed 1960s activists were quietly resurrected under other names. Paramilitary SWAT teams and tactical squads were formed, along with highly politicized "community relations" and "beat rep" programs featuring conspicuous Black, Latin, and female officers. Generous federal funding and sophisticated technology became available through the Law Enforcement Assistance Administration, while FBI-led "joint anti-terrorist task forces" introduced a new level of inter-agency coordination.[40]

Meanwhile, the CIA continued to use university professors, journalists, labor leaders, publishing houses, cultural organizations, and philanthropic fronts to mold U.S. public opinion.[41] At the same time, Army Special Forces and other elite military units began to train local police for counter-insurgency and to intensify their own preparations, following the guidelines of the secret Pentagon contingency plans, "Garden Plot" and "Cable Splicer." They drew increasingly on manuals based on the British colonial experience in Kenya and Northern Ireland, which teach the essential methodology of COINTELPRO under the rubric of "low-intensity warfare," and stress early intervention to neutralize potential opposition before it can take hold.[42]

While domestic covert operations were scaled down once the 1960s upsurge had subsided (thanks in part to the success of COINTELPRO), they did not stop. In its April 27, 1971 directives disbanding COINTELPRO, the FBI provided for future covert action to continue "with tight procedures to ensure absolute security."[43] The results are apparent in the record of 1970s covert operations which have so far come to light:

The celebration of the bicentennial of the Constitution is happening here in Philadelphia.

So, to be cautious, we infiltrated a few political groups.

And now the press is making a big deal about it, though frankly I don't know why.

I mean, we're protecting the right to not be bothered by fringe groups who want to put a damper on the celebration.

We're protecting the right to be safe from terrorist priests and anti-nuclear homosexuals.

And besides... we coulda just dropped a bomb.

The Native American Movement: 1970s FBI attacks on resurgent Native American resistance have been well documented by Ward Churchill and others.[44] In 1973, the Bureau led a paramilitary invasion of the Pine Ridge Reservation in South Dakota as American Indian Movement (AIM) activists gathered there for symbolic protests at Wounded Knee, the site of an earlier U.S. massacre of Native Americans. The FBI directed the entire 71-day siege, deploying federal marshals, U.S. Army personnel, Bureau of Indian Affairs police, local GOONs (Guardians of the Oglala Nation, an armed tribal vigilante force), and a vast array of heavy weaponry.

In the following years, the FBI and its allies waged all-out war on AIM and the Native people. From 1973-76, they killed 69 residents of the tiny Pine Ridge reservation, a rate of political murder comparable to the first years of the Pinochet regime in Chile.[45] To justify such a reign of terror and undercut public protest against it, the Bureau launched a complementary program of psychological warfare.

Central to this effort was a carefully orchestrated campaign to reinforce the already deeply ingrained myth of the "Indian savage." In one operation, the FBI fabricated reports that AIM "Dog Soldiers" planned widespread "sniping at tourists" and "burning of farmers" in South Dakota. The son of liberal U.S. Senator (and Arab-American activist) James Abourezk, was named as a "gunrunner," and the Bureau issued a nationwide alert picked up by media across the country.

To the same end, FBI undercover operatives framed AIM members Paul "Skyhorse" Durant and Richard "Mohawk" Billings for the brutal murder of a Los Angeles taxi driver. A bogus AIM note taking credit for the killing was found pinned to a signpost near the murder site, along with a bundle of hair said to be the victim's "scalp." Newspaper headlines screamed of "ritual murder" by "radical Indians." By the time the defendants were finally cleared of the spurious charges, many of AIM's main financial backers had been scared away and its work among a major urban concentration of Native people was in ruin.

In March 1975, a central perpetrator of this hoax, AIM's national security chief Doug Durham, was unmasked as an undercover operative for the FBI. As AIM's liaison with the Wounded Knee Legal Defense/Offense Committee during the trials of Dennis Banks and other Native American leaders, Durham had routinely participated in confidential strategy sessions. He confessed to stealing organizational funds during his two years with AIM, and to setting up the arrest of AIM militants for actions he had organized. It was Durham who authored the AIM documents that the FBI consistently cited to demonstrate the group's supposed violent tendencies.

Prompted by Durham's revelations, the Senate Intelligence Committee announced on June 23, 1975 that it would hold public hearings on FBI operations against AIM. Three days later, armed FBI agents assaulted an AIM house on the Pine Ridge reservation. When the smoke cleared, AIM activist Joe Stuntz Killsright and two FBI agents lay dead. The media, barred from the scene "to preserve the evidence," broadcast the Bureau's false accounts of a bloody "Indian ambush," and the congressional hearings were quietly cancelled.

The FBI was then free to crush AIM and clear out the last pockets of resistance at Pine Ridge. It launched what the Chairman of the U.S. Civil Rights Commission described as "a full-scale military-type invasion of the reservation"[46] complete with M-16s, Huey helicopters, tracking dogs, and armored personnel carriers. Eventually AIM leader Leonard Peltier was tried for the agents' deaths before a right-wing judge who met secretly with the FBI. AIM member Anna Mae Aquash was found murdered after FBI agents threatened to kill her unless she helped them to frame Peltier. Peltier's conviction, based on perjured testimony and falsified FBI ballistics evidence, was upheld on appeal. (The panel of federal judges included William Webster until the very day of his official appointment as Director of the FBI.) Despite mounting evidence of impropriety in Peltier's trial, and Amnesty International's call for a review of his case, the Native American leader remains in maximum security prison.

The Black Movement: Government covert action against Black activists also continued in the 1970s. Targets ranged from community-based groups to the Provisional Government of the Republic of New Afrika and the surviving remnants of the Black Panther Party.

In Mississippi, federal and state agents attempted to discredit and disrupt the United League of Marshall County, a broad-based grassroots civil rights group struggling to stop Klan violence. In California, a notorious paid operative for the FBI, Darthard Perry, code-named "Othello," infiltrated and disrupted local Black groups and took personal credit for the fire that razed the Watts Writers Workshop's multi-million dollar cultural center in Los Angeles in 1973. The Los Angeles Police Department later admitted infiltrating at least seven 1970s community groups, including the Black-led Coalition Against Police Abuse.[47]

In the mid-1970s, the U.S. Bureau of Alcohol, Tobacco and Firearms (ATF) conspired with the Wilmington, North Carolina police to frame nine local civil rights workers and the Rev. Ben Chavis, field organizer for the Commission for Racial Justice of the United Church of Christ. Chavis had been sent to North Carolina to help Black communities respond to escalating racist violence against school desegregation. Instead of arresting Klansmen, the ATF and police coerced three young Black prisoners into falsely accusing Chavis and the others of burning white-owned property. Although all three prisoners later admitted they had lied in response to official threats and bribes, the FBI found no impropriety. The courts repeatedly refused to reopen the case and the Wilmington Ten served many years in prison before pressure from international religious and human rights groups won their release.[48]

As the Republic of New Afrika (RNA) began to build autonomous Black economic and political institutions in the deep South, the Bureau repeatedly disrupted its meetings and blocked its attempts to buy land. On August 18, 1971, four months after the supposed end of COINTELPRO, the FBI and police launched an armed pre-dawn assault on national RNA offices in Jackson, Mississippi. Carrying a warrant for a fugitive who had been brought to RNA Headquarters by FBI informer Thomas Spells, the attackers concentrated their fire where the informer's floor plan indicated that RNA President Imari Obadele slept. Though Obadele was away at the time of the raid, the Bureau had him arrested and imprisoned on charges of conspiracy to assault a government agent.[49]

The COINTELPRO-triggered collapse of the Black Panthers' organization and support in the winter of 1971 left them defenseless as the government moved to prevent them from regrouping. On August 21, 1971, national Party officer George Jackson, world-renowned author of the political autobiography *Soledad Brother,* was murdered by San Quentin prison authorities on the pretext of an attempted jailbreak.[50] In July 1972, Southern California Panther leader Elmer "Geronimo" Pratt was successfully framed for a senseless $70 robbery-murder committed while he was hundreds of miles away in Oakland, California, attending Black Panther meetings for which the FBI managed to "lose" all of its surveillance records. Documents obtained through the Freedom of Information Act later revealed that at least two FBI agents had infiltrated Pratt's defense committee. They also indicated that the state's main witness, Julio Butler, was a paid informer who had worked in the Party under the direction of the FBI and the Los Angeles Police Department. For many years, FBI Director Webster publicly denied that Pratt had ever been a COINTELPRO target, despite the documentary proof in his own agency's records.[51]

Also targeted well into the 1970s were former Panthers assigned to form an underground to defend against armed government attack on the Party. It was they who had regrouped as the Black Liberation Army (BLA) when the Party was destroyed. FBI files show that, within a month of the close of COINTELPRO, further Bureau operations against the BLA were mapped out in secret meetings convened by presidential aide John Ehrlichman and attended by President Nixon and Attorney General Mitchell. In the following years, many former Panther leaders were murdered by the police in supposed "shoot-outs" with the BLA. Others, such as Sundiata Acoli, Assata Shakur, Dhoruba Al-Mujahid Bin Wahad (formerly Richard Moore), and the New York 3 (Herman Bell, Anthony "Jalil" Bottom, and Albert "Nuh" Washington) were sentenced to long prison terms after rigged trials.[52]

In the case of the New York 3, FBI ballistics reports withheld during their mid-1970s trials show that bullets from an alleged murder weapon did not match those found at the site of the killings for which they are still serving life terms. The star witness against them has publicly recanted his testimony, swearing that he lied after being tortured by police (who repeatedly jammed an electric cattleprod into his testicles) and secretly threatened by the prosecutor and judge. The same judge later dismissed petitions to reopen the case, refusing to hold any hearing or to disqualify himself, even though his misconduct is a major issue. As the NY3 continued to press for a new trial, their evidence was ignored by the news media while their former prosecutor's one-sided, racist "docudrama" on the case, *Badge of the Assassin,* aired on national television.[53]

The Chicano and Puerto Rican Movements: From 1972-1974, La Raza Unida Party of Texas was plagued with repeated, unsolved COINTELPRO-style political break-ins.[54] Former government operative Eustacio "Frank" Martínez has admitted that after the close of COIN-TELPRO, the U.S. Bureau of Alcohol, Tobacco, and Firearms (ATF) paid him to help destroy La Casa de Carnalísimo, a Chicano community anti-drug program in Los Angeles. Martínez, who had previously infiltrated the Brown Berets and the Chicano Moratorium, stated that the ATF directed him to provoke bombings and plant a drug pusher in La Casa.[55]

In 1973, Chicano activist and lawyer Francisco "Kiko" Martínez was indicted in Colorado on trumped-up bombing charges and suspended from the bar. He was forced to leave the United States for fear of assassination by police directed to shoot him "on sight." When Martínez was eventually brought to trial in the 1980s, many of the charges against him were dropped for insufficient evidence and local juries acquitted him of others. One case ended in a mistrial when it was found that the judge had met secretly with prosecutors, police, and government witnesses to plan perjured testimony, and had conspired with the FBI to conceal video cameras in the courtroom.[56]

Starting in 1976, the FBI manipulated the grand jury process to assault both the Chicano and Puerto Rican movements. Under the guise of investigating Las Fuerzas Armadas de Liberación National Puertorriqueño (FALN) and other Puerto Rican urban guerrillas, the Bureau harassed and disrupted a cultural center, an alternative high school, and other promising community organizing efforts in Chicago's Puerto Rican barrio and in the Chicano communities of Denver and northern New Mexico. It subpoenaed radical Puerto Rican trade union leader Federico Cintrón Fiallo and key staff of the National Commission on Hispanic Affairs of the U.S. Episcopal Church to appear before federal grand juries and jailed them for refusing to cooperate. The independent labor movement in Puerto Rico and the Commission's important work in support of Puerto Rican and Chicano organizing were effectively discredited.[57]

On July 25, 1978, an undercover agent lured two young Puerto Rican independence activists, Carlos Soto Arriví and Arnaldo Darío Rosado, to their deaths in a police ambush at Cerro Maravilla, Puerto Rico. The agent, Alejandro González Malavé, worked under the direct supervision of the FBI-trained intelligence chief of the island's police force. The FBI refused to investigate when the police claimed they were merely returning gunfire initiated by the activists. Later it was proved that Soto and Darío had surrendered and were then beaten and shot dead while on their knees. Though a number of officers were found guilty of perjury in the cover-up and one was sentenced for the murder, the officials who set up the operation remain free. González has been promoted.[58]

On November 11, 1979, Angel Rodríguez Cristóbal, popular socialist leader of the movement to stop U.S. Navy bombing practice on the inhabited Puerto Rican island of Vieques, was murdered in the U.S. penitentiary in Tallahassee, Florida. Though U.S. authorities claimed "suicide," Rodríguez Cristóbal, in the second month of a six-month term for civil disobedience, had been in good spirits when seen by his lawyer hours before his death. He had been subjected to continuous threats and harassment, including forced drugging and isolation, during his confinement. Though he was said to have been found hanging by a bed sheet, there was a large gash on his forehead and blood on the floor of his cell.[59]

The Women's, Gay, and Lesbian Movements: FBI documents show that the women's liberation movement remained a major target of covert operations throughout the 1970s. Long after the official end of COINTELPRO, the Bureau continued to infiltrate and disrupt feminist organizations, publications, and projects. Its view of the women's movement is revealed by a 1973 report listing the national women's

newspaper *off our backs* as "ARMED AND DANGEROUS—EX-
TREMIST."[60]

Covert operations also continued against lesbian and gay organizing. One former FBI informer, Earl Robert "Butch" Merritt, revealed that
from October 1971 through June 1972 he received a weekly stipend to
infiltrate gay publications and organizations in the District of Columbia.
He was ordered to conduct break-ins, spread false rumors that certain
gay activists were actually police or FBI informants, and create racial
dissension between and within groups. One assignment involved calling
Black groups to tell them they would not be welcome at Gay Activists
Alliance and Gay Liberation Front meetings.[61]

As in the case of the Puerto Rican and Chicano movements,
criminal investigations provided a convenient pretext for escalated FBI
attacks on lesbian and feminist activists in the mid-1970s. In purported
pursuit of anti-war fugitives Susan Saxe and Kathy Powers, FBI agents
flooded the women's communities of Boston, Philadelphia, Lexington
(Kentucky), Hartford and New Haven. Their conspicuous interrogation
of hundreds of politically active women, followed by highly publicized
grand jury subpoenas and jailings, wreaked havoc in health collectives
and other vital projects. Activists and potential supporters were scared
off, and fear spread across the country, hampering women's and lesbian
organizing nationally.[62]

The Anti-war and New Left Movements: Government covert
action against the New Left and anti-war movements also persisted,
especially as activists mobilized to protest the 1972 Republican and
Democratic Party conventions. In San Diego, where the Republicans
initially planned to convene, this campaign culminated in the January 6,
1972 attempt on the life of anti-convention organizer Peter Bohmer by
a "Secret Army Organization" of ex-Minutemen formed, subsidized,
armed, and protected by the FBI.[63]

Movement organizing and government sabotage continued when
the Republican convention was moved to Miami Beach, Florida. In May
1972, Bill Lemmer, Southern Regional Coordinator of Vietnam Veterans
Against the War (VVAW), a key group in the convention protest coalition, surfaced as an undercover FBI operative. Lemmer's false testimony
enabled the Bureau to haul the VVAW's national leadership before a
grand jury hundreds of miles away during the week of the convention.[64]

FBI efforts to put the VVAW "out of business" were later confirmed
by another ex-operative. Joe Burton of Tampa, Florida, told the *New York
Times* "that between 1972 and 1974 he worked as a paid FBI operative
assigned to infiltrate and disrupt various radical groups in this country
and Canada." Burton described how specialists were flown in from FBI

Headquarters to help him forge bogus documents and "establish a 'sham' political group, 'the Red Star Cadre,' for disruptive purposes."[65]

The same article reported that "two other former FBI operatives, Harry E. Schafer, 3d, and his wife, Jill, told of similar disruptive activity they undertook at the bureau's direction during the same period." Working out of "a similar bogus New Orleans front group, termed the 'Red Collective,'" the Schafers boasted of diverting substantial funds which had been raised to support the American Indian Movement.

The Labor Movement: One of *agent provocateur* Joe Burton's main targets was the United Electrical Workers Union (UE). The FBI falsified records to get Burton into UE Tampa Local 1201 soon after its successful 1973 organizing drive upset the Westinghouse Corporation's plan to develop a chain of non-union plants in the South. Burton's attacks on genuine activists repeatedly disrupted UE meetings. His ultra-left proclamations in the union's name antagonized newly organized workers and gave credibility to the company's red-baiting. Burton also helped the FBI move against the United Farm Workers and the American Federation of State, County, and Municipal Employees (AFSCME).[66]

In the mid-1970s, the FBI was instrumental in covering up the murder of labor activist Karen Silkwood and the theft of her files documenting the radioactive contamination of workers at the Kerr-McGee nuclear fuel plant near Oklahoma City. Silkwood, elected to the Oil, Chemical, and Atomic Workers local bargaining committee, had amassed proof that the company was falsifying safety reports to hide widespread exposure to dangerous levels of highly carcinogenic plutonium. She was killed when her car crashed into a concrete embankment en route to a November 13, 1974 meeting with *New York Times* reporter David Burnham. Her files were never recovered from the wreck. While prominent independent experts concluded that Silkwood's car was bumped from behind and forced off the road, the FBI found that she fell asleep at the wheel after overdosing on quaaludes and that she never had any files. It quickly closed the case, and helped Kerr-McGee sabotage congressional investigations and posthumously slander Silkwood as a mentally unstable drug addict. Key to the smear campaign were articles and testimony by Jacque Srouji, a Tennessee journalist secretly in the employ of the FBI, who later confessed to having served in a long string of 1960s COINTELPRO operations.[67]

In 1979, government operatives played key roles in the massacre of communist labor organizers during a multi-racial anti-Klan march in Greensboro, North Carolina. Heading the KKK/Nazi death squad was Ed Dawson, a long-time paid FBI/police informer in the Klan. Leading the local American Nazi Party branch into Dawson's "United Racist Front" was U.S. Bureau of Alcohol, Tobacco, and Firearms undercover agent Bernard Butkovich. Though their controlling agencies were fully warned of the Front's murderous plans, they did nothing to protect the demonstrators. Instead, the police gave Dawson a copy of the march route and withdrew as his caravan moved in for the kill. Dawson's sharpshooters carefully picked off key cadre of the Communist Workers Party (CWP), including the president and president-elect of two Amalgamated Clothing and Textile Workers Union locals, an organizer at a third local mill, and a leader of AFSCME's organizing drive at a nearby medical center. In the aftermath, the FBI attempted to cover up the government's role and to put the blame on the CWP.[68]

At the turn of the decade, the Bureau joined with Naval Intelligence and the San Diego Police to neutralize a militant multi-racial union at the shipyards of the National Steel and Shipbuilding Company, a major U.S. naval contractor. The Bureau paid Ramon Barton to infiltrate Ironworkers Local 627 when it elected leftist officers and began to publicly protest dangerous working conditions. After an explosion from a gas leak killed two workers, Barton lured three others into helping him build a bomb and transport it in his van, where they were arrested. Though the workers entrapped by Barton were not union officials and were acquitted of most charges by a San Diego jury, the Ironworkers International used their trial as a pretext for placing the local in trusteeship and expelling its elected officers.[69]

• Domestic Covert Action Has Persisted Throughout the 1980s

All this and more occurred during a period of liberal reform, when political activism had somewhat subsided. The 1980s, by contrast, have been marked by the rise of right-wing political power and new forms of popular opposition to reactionary government policy. Under these conditions, the danger of domestic covert action is greater than ever.

One indication of the severity of the current threat is the level of recent political repression. The incidents reviewed in the Introduction are marked by the kind of blatant harassment that was consistently used in conjunction with COINTELPRO: offices of churches and groups opposing U.S. Central America policy conspicuously burglarized; personal papers of international travelers confiscated by U.S. customs upon their return at the border; dissidents facing deportation for their political views; activists hounded at their jobs and in their communities, hauled before grand juries, and arrested and jailed on false charges.

Even more alarming is the amount of current covert activity that has come to light. Since the vast majority of COINTELPRO-type operations stay hidden until long after the damage has been done, those we are already aware of represent only the tip of the iceberg. Far more is sure to lurk beneath the surface.

Most of today's domestic covert action can be kept concealed because full government secrecy has been restored. The Freedom of Information Act, a source of major disclosures about COINTELPRO, was drastically narrowed in the 1980s through administrative and judicial reinterpretation as well as legislative amendment. Thousands of government files were shielded from public scrutiny under presidential directives that vastly expand the range of information classified "top-secret." Government employees now face censorship even after they retire, and new laws make it a federal crime to disclose "any information that identifies an individual as a covert agent."[70]

While restoring full secrecy, the Reagan administration invested covert action with a new legitimacy. In the past, such operations were acknowledged to be improper and illegal. The Senate Intelligence Committee condemned COINTELPRO as "a sophisticated vigilante operation aimed squarely at preventing the exercise of First Amendment rights of speech and association."[71] From its inception, the CIA was barred by law from performing "internal security functions."[72] Top government officials took care to insulate themselves so they could deny involvement if an unseemly operation came to light. These conditions established a kind of speed limit, a set of restrictions which the agencies felt free to exceed, but only by a certain margin.

In the 1980s even this ceiling was lifted. Reagan and his cohorts openly embraced the use of covert operations at home and abroad. They endorsed such action, legalized it, sponsored it, and raised it to the level of patriotic virtue.

Within months of taking office, Reagan pardoned W. Mark Felt and Edward S. Miller, the only FBI officials convicted of COINTELPRO crimes. His congressional allies publicly honored these criminals and praised their work.[73] The President continually revived the tired old Red Scare, adding a new "terrorist" bogeyman, while Attorney General Meese campaigned to narrow the scope of the Bill of Rights and limit judicial review of the constitutionality of government action.

From the National Security Council's offices in the White House basement, Lt. Col. Oliver North proudly funded and orchestrated break-ins and other "dirty tricks" to defeat congressional critics of U.S. policy in Central America and neutralize grassroots protest. He ran elaborate networks of paper organizations set up by former government covert operatives who regrouped to do the same work for more money in the "private sector." Special Prosecutor Walsh found evidence that North and Retired Air Force Gen. Richard Secord (architect of 1960s U.S. covert action in Cambodia) used Iran-Contra funds to harass the Christic Institute, a church-funded public interest law group which specializes in exposing government misconduct.[74] North also helped Reagan's cronies at the Federal Emergency Management Administration develop contingency plans for suspending the Constitution, establishing martial law, and holding political dissidents in concentration camps in the event of "national opposition against a U.S. military invasion abroad."[75]

Much of what was done outside the law under COINTELPRO has since been legalized by Executive Order No. 12333 (December 4, 1981) and new Attorney General's "Guidelines on General Crimes, Racketeering Enterprise and Domestic Security/Terrorism Investigations" (March 7, 1983). For the first time in U.S. history. government infiltration "for the purpose of influencing the activity of" domestic political organizations has received official sanction (E.O.12333, §2.9). This prerogative is now extended to the FBI and anyone acting on its behalf. It provided a legal pretext for the Bureau's attacks on CISPES and other opponents of U.S. policy in Central America.

The new executive order asserts the President's right to authorize CIA "special activities" (the official euphemism for covert operations) redefined to include activity *anywhere* "in support of national foreign policy objectives abroad" (§1.8(e), §3.4(h)). It legalizes "counterintelligence activities...within the United States" on the part of the FBI and the CIA, Army, Navy, Air Force, and Marines (§1.8(c), §1.12(d)). "Specialized equipment, technical knowledge, or assistance of expert personnel" may be provided by any of these agencies "to support local law enforcement" (§2.6c). All are free to mount electronic and mail surveillance without a warrant, and the FBI may also conduct warrantless "unconsented physical searches" (break-ins) if the Attorney General finds probable cause to believe the action is "directed against a foreign power or an agent of a foreign power" (§2.4, §2.5). This signals open season on CISPES, sanctuary churches, anti-apartheid groups, and anyone else who maintains friendly relations with a country or movement opposed by the administration or who dares to organize protest against U.S. foreign policy.

Given how much is at stake, we can hardly afford to ignore these many signs of danger. The FBI and police have now been fully rehabilitated. The CIA and military have assumed an expanded homefront role. Covert action has been legalized and endorsed at the highest levels of government. Official secrecy has been restored.

They say COINTELPRO is dead, and has been for years.

But I don't know.

What about the FBI infiltration into the Sanctuary Movement?

What about their investigation of Physicians for Social Responsibility?

What about the continued break-ins into offices of Central American organizations?

If COINTELPRO is dead, then J. Edgar Hoover lives.

© oikesguich 1/87

Government harassment of domestic dissidents continues unabated. Evidence of current infiltration and clandestine disruption is surfacing at an alarming rate. Taken together, these developments leave us only one safe assumption: full-scale covert operations are already underway to neutralize today's opposition movements before they can reach the massive level of the 1960s.

• Domestic Covert Action Has Become a Permanent Feature of U.S. Government

So long as conservative Republicans remain in power, there is no reason to expect this threat to subside. But what if liberal Democrats were in control? Recent U.S. history indicates that so far as covert operations are concerned, the difference would be marginal at best.

The record of the past 50 years reveals a pattern of continuous domestic covert action. Its use has been documented in each of the last nine administrations, Democratic as well as Republican. FBI testimony shows "COINTELPRO tactics" already in full swing during the presidencies of Democrats Franklin Delano Roosevelt and Harry Truman.[76] COINTELPRO itself, while initiated under Eisenhower, grew from one program to six under the Democratic administrations of Kennedy and Johnson. It flourished when an outspoken liberal, Ramsey Clark, was Attorney General (1966-1968). After COINTELPRO was exposed, similar programs continued under other names during the Carter years as well as under Nixon, Ford, and Reagan. They have outlived J. Edgar Hoover and remained in place under all of his successors.

Covert police methods have been used against progressive social movements since the founding of the country. Undercover operatives disrupted the historic efforts of rebel slaves and Native American, Mexican, and Puerto Rican resistance. Dissident journalists, insurgent workers, and rebellious farmers were arrested on false charges and jailed or hung after rigged trials.[77]

Through most of U.S. history, progressive activists faced the blatant brutality of hired thugs and right-wing vigilantes backed by government troops. As the country grew more urban and industrial, newly formed municipal police forces came to play a greater role. By the turn of this century, local police departments were running massive anti-union operations in collaboration with the Pinkertons and other private detective agencies.[78]

With World War I and the increasing national integration of the U.S. political economy, the federal government began to take more responsibility for control of domestic dissent. From 1917 on, the Justice Department's Bureau of Investigation, forerunner of the FBI, coordinated its work closely with a 250,000 member right-wing vigilante group, the American Protective League. Together they mounted nationwide raids, arrests, and prosecutions which jailed thousands of draft resisters and labor activists and destroyed the Industrial Workers of the World (IWW, or "Wobblies").[79] Following the Russian Revolution, the Bureau helped foment the Red Scare of 1919-20. J. Edgar Hoover took personal responsibility for deporting "Red Emma" Goldman and directing the Palmer Raids in which thousands of progressive immigrants were rounded up, jailed, and brutalized, and hundreds were deported.[80]

Stung by public criticism of these raids, Hoover switched to more covert methods in the early 1920s. His men infiltrated the ranks of striking railway workers and penetrated the Sacco-Vanzetti Defense Committee to steal funds raised to support the indicted anarchists.[81] In an operation that prefigured COINTELPRO, Hoover masterminded the destruction of the main Black movement of the post-World War I period, Marcus Garvey's Universal Negro Improvement Association (UNIA). His agents penetrated the multi-million member UNIA and set up the federal mail fraud conviction that discredited its charismatic leader, leading to Garvey's deportation and the group's collapse.[82]

Through the rest of the 1920s, the Bureau kept a low profile as domestic insurgency subsided. In the early years of the Depression, primary responsibility for policing dissent remained in the hands of local law enforcement agencies, private detectives, and right-wing groups such as the American Legion. Meanwhile, Hoover and the FBI rose to national prominence by leading a widely heralded "War on Crime." Their capture of John Dillinger and other notorious desperados made headlines across the country. The Bureau was glorified in Hollywood films and an immensely popular radio series. The media portrayed the FBI as invincible and proclaimed J. Edgar Hoover "Public Hero Number One."[83]

This new stature positioned the Bureau to regain its status as the nation's political police. In 1936, it won secret authorization to once again target "subversive activities in the United States." In a memo to his subordinates, Hoover attributed this coup to confidential "information" he had presented to President Roosevelt showing that "the Communists...practically controlled" at least one key industrial union and were moving to "get control of" others.[84]

The FBI vastly expanded its operations during World War II and acquired new covert technology, including the capacity for expert forgery. In the aftermath of the war, as the United States began to exercise hegemonic world power and to identify the Soviet Union as its main enemy, the Bureau firmly established its political role as an accepted institutional reality. The Senate Intelligence Committee later found that it was in this period, well before the start of COINTELPRO, that "the domestic intelligence programs of the FBI...became permanent features of government."[85]

The Committee attributes the Bureau's ability to consolidate political police powers to the "Cold War fears" which swept the country during the late 1940s and the 1950s, but it skips over the Bureau's central role in fomenting those fears. FBI Director Hoover openly threw his enormous public prestige behind the postwar witchhunts mounted by the House Un-American Activities Committee (HUAC) and Joseph McCarthy's Senate Internal Security Sub-Committee. Directed by law to investigate the loyalty of federal employees, the FBI secretly passed confidential raw files to its congressional allies, especially McCarthy and the rising young star of HUAC, Richard Nixon.[86]

Above all, Hoover and his men set up and orchestrated the pivotal spy trials that made the witchhunts credible. In 1950, former high-ranking State Department official Alger Hiss, President of the Carnegie Endowment for International Peace, was found guilty of perjury for denying that he had copied confidential government papers for the Soviet Union in the late 1930s. In 1951, U.S. communists Ethel and Julius Rosenberg and Morton Sobell were convicted, and the Rosenbergs executed, for allegedly passing to the Soviet Union "atomic secrets" that were already general scientific knowledge. In each case, the star witness was an informer whose initial contradictory accounts were meshed into semi-coherent testimony only after months of careful FBI coaching. In each, the supposedly incorruptible FBI vouched for the authenticity of key documentary evidence which activists later learned could easily have been forged.[87]

Subsequent investigation and analysis suggest that both cases may well have been fabricated. At the time, however, their impact was devastating. By appearing to validate the witchhunts, they paved the way for the purge of an entire generation of radicals from U.S. political and cultural life.

In this atmosphere of anti-communist hysteria, as in the preceding years of wartime fear of espionage, the FBI was free to move against a broad range of domestic political movements. It took an occasional swipe at the right wing and managed to arrest a few outright Nazi saboteurs. As always, however, the brunt of its attack was directed against those who sought progressive social change.

The Senate Intelligence Committee documented long-standing, pre-COINTELPRO FBI infiltration of industrial unions, major Black or-

ganizations (including the NAACP and the Nation of Islam), the un-
employed movement, the Nationalist Party of Puerto Rico, and at least
one group of reform Democrats (the Independent Voters of Illinois).[88]
Documents later obtained under the Freedom of Information Act reveal
FBI undercover operations in the late 1940s against the third party
presidential candidacy of former Vice President Henry Wallace, the
pro-Wallace American Labor Party (ALP), and U.S. Congressman Vito
Marcantonio (D/ALP-NY).[89] Other Bureau memoranda show the collaboration of Ronald Reagan, "Confidential Informant T-10," in FBI
maneuvers to oust leftists from the Screen Actors Guild and the Hollywood film industry.[90] Bureau targets during the late 1940s and early
1950s also included the National Lawyers Guild and the American
Friends Service Committee, as well as the Mattachine Society, the
Daughters of Bilitis, and other early gay and lesbian rights groups.[91]

From the outset, these groups faced far more than mere surveillance. From 1936-56, the FBI took advantage of wartime fears and
postwar hysteria to slip into place the domestic covert operations later
consolidated under COINTELPRO. Ex-agents' report that activists'
homes and offices were routinely burglarized during these years.[92] As
early as 1939, the Bureau began to compile a secret "Security Index"
listing subversives to be detained in the event of a "national emergency."[93] William Sullivan, former head of the FBI Intelligence Division,
testified that, "We were engaged in COINTELPRO tactics, to divide,
confuse, weaken, in diverse ways, an organization. We were engaged
in that when I entered the Bureau in 1941."[94] The Senate Intelligence
Committee found that by 1946 the Bureau had a "policy" of preparing
and disseminating "propaganda" to "discredit" its targets.[95]

Thus, COINTELPRO was not a radical departure. It merely centralized and intensified long-standing FBI policy and practice. The 1956
directive setting up the new program took as its starting point the historic
record of Bureau work "to foster factionalism, bring the Communist Party
and its leaders into disrepute before the American public, and cause
confusion and dissatisfaction among rank-and-file members." It called
for a better coordinated, more focused, "all-out disruptive attack" to
make up for new judicial restrictions on political prosecutions and to
eliminate once and for all a U.S. left already in disarray.[96]

Conceived as a mid-1950s *coup de grace* against a failing Old Left,
COINTELPRO became the cutting edge of the Bureau's attack on the
rising struggles of the 1960s. It provided the framework for operations
against the resurgent Black movement whose first audible rumblings, in
the 1955 Montgomery, Alabama bus boycott, may explain the urgency
of the Bureau's drive to do away with what remained of an organized

radical presence in the United States. It also formed the FBI's primary response to the student and anti-war protests which swept the country during the 1960s.

COINTELPRO grew increasingly important as the traditional modes of repression failed. An undaunted new generation of activists made a laughing stock of HUAC and turned criminal trials into political forums. Although brute force ultimately did contribute to their demise, for most of the decade police beatings served only to stiffen resistance and to help win over the millions who watched on television.

Reviewing the Bureau's experience with domestic covert action as of 1964, J. Edgar Hoover concluded that:

> These ideas will not be increased in number or improved upon from the standpoint of accomplishments merely through the institution of a program such as COINTELPRO which is given another name, and which, in fact, only encompasses everything that has been done in the past or will be done in the future.[97]

True to his words, Hoover did continue domestic covert action under "another name" when he eventually had to shut down COINTELPRO. Fearing public exposure, the FBI reverted to the less centralized, more secure procedures of the previous era, but the basic approach persisted.

Over the past 50 years, clandestine work has become an essential part of the Bureau's mode of operation. Many of its senior agents are now specialists whose professional advancement requires that the government continue to rely on covert action. A similar group of "old hands" has emerged from the covert operations that the United States and its European allies developed in an effort to maintain control of their colonies and neo-colonies in countries such as Algeria, the Congo, India, Northern Ireland, Chile, and Vietnam. With Hoover's death and Webster's ascendancy at the FBI and then the CIA, the two sets of spies came gradually to coordinate and integrate their work.

The combined experience of these veteran covert operatives has given rise to a growing literature and theory of counter-insurgency. Their widely circulated texts and manuals restate the basic precepts of COIN-TELPRO and pound home the necessity for continuous covert operations. The leading treatise, *Low-Intensity Operations: Subversion, Insurgency, and Peacekeeping,* by Frank Kitson, British commander in Kenya, Malaysia, Cyprus, and Northern Ireland, insists that infiltration and "psychological operations" be mounted against dissident groups in "normal times," before any mass movement can develop.[98]

Careerism, old boy networks, theories, and treatises help to perpetuate domestic covert action. The persistence of such operations can be fully explained, however, only in terms of their value to economic and political elites. Any social order based on inequality of wealth and power depends, to some degree, on political repression to control the disadvantaged majority. Modern U.S. elites have particular need for covert measures because the war at home is primarily the responsibility of the federal government, a government which is under intense pressure to appear to be democratic.

The federal government has become the main arm of domestic repression through a series of historic developments. First, internal political conflict has come to focus increasingly on issues of public policy. Second, business and industry, which once played a major role, now rely on the public sector for unprofitable support services—from post offices, airports, roads, and job training to the pacification of workers and markets at home and abroad. They are no longer willing to maintain a large-scale in-house apparatus for repressing societal political dissent or to purchase such services from private agencies. Finally, state and local governments lack the funds and personnel to cope with countrywide dissident movements. Federal coordination and direction is demanded by the national integration of the U.S. economy and culture, with its geographically mobile population and instant communication.

For all these reasons, U.S. domestic political repression is now effectively nationalized. Local police may still be the foot soldiers for many arrests, raids, beatings, and infiltrations; college administrators, corporate security forces, and private right-wing groups may also help out. But when it comes to full-scale strategic, coordinated domestic counter-insurgency, only "the Feds" can do the job.

But the federal government has other imperatives. It strives to maintain U.S. control over world markets and resources in an era when most of Asia, Africa, and Latin America have been legally decolonized. It competes internationally with the Soviet Union, Germany, and Japan. At the same time, it needs patriotic support, or at least passive acquiescence, at home. For all these purposes, it must effectively promote the image of the United States as leader of the "free world," complete with free speech and the rule of law.

If the U.S. government is seen as unduly repressive within its own borders, however, it will have trouble maintaining the allegiance of its citizenry and competing effectively for world influence. It can sustain its legitimacy, while effectively marginalizing or eliminating domestic dissent, if it makes the victims of official violence appear to be the aggressors and provokes dissident movements to tear themselves apart through factionalism and other modes of self-destruction. No wonder covert action is here to stay.

What We Can Do About Domestic Covert Action

We obviously cannot stop domestic covert action simply by electing better public officials, passing stronger laws, or winning court cases. Clandestine repression will end only with the elimination of the race, gender, class, and international domination it serves to uphold. Meanwhile, it severely undermines our ability to build the broad-based movements needed to win fundamental change. To organize and sustain such movements, we have to learn how to deal with domestic covert action in a way that minimizes its interference with our work.

There are two complementary means to this end. The first approach requires work within our movements. It is essential that we learn to recognize the methods of covert action and take steps to reduce their impact on our work. The second approach involves organizing publicly to expose and oppose the government's continued reliance on those methods. Though domestic covert action cannot be eliminated without more systemic change, we do have the capacity to substantially limit and weaken it.

• Learning the Methods of COINTELPRO and How to Protect Ourselves Against Them

Though the details of future covert action will be adapted to changing social and technological conditions, only a limited number of basic methods and approaches exist. Like chess masters and military strategists who hone their skills by replaying old contests, we can improve our ability to defend against these modes of attack through close study of recent history. If we understand how the FBI and police moved in the past, we will be better able to recognize and avoid their future tricks and traps. If we grasp the mistakes of earlier movements, we can take essential precautions now without encouraging paranoia or diverting attention from our main goals.

A CHECKLIST OF ESSENTIAL PRECAUTIONS

1. Check out the authenticity of any disturbing letter, rumor, phone call, or other communication before acting on it. Ask the supposed source if she or he is responsible.

2. Keep records of incidents which appear to reflect COINTELPRO-type activity. Evaluate your response and report your experiences to the Movement Support Network and other groups that document repression and resistance around the country. (See page 92.)

3. Deal openly and honestly with the differences within our movements (race, gender, class, age, religion, national origin, sexual orientation, personality, experience, physical and intellectual capacities, etc.) before the FBI and police can exploit them.

4. Don't try to expose a suspected agent or informer without solid proof. Purges based on mere suspicion only help the FBI and police create distrust and paranoia. It generally works better to criticize what a disruptive person says and does, without speculating as to why.

5. Support all movement activists who come under government attack. Don't be put off by political slander, such as recent attempts to smear some militant opponents of government policy as "terrorists." Organize public opposition to all FBI witchhunts, grand jury subpoenas, political trials, and other forms of government and right-wing harassment.

6. Cultivate relationships with sympathetic journalists who seem willing to investigate and publicize domestic covert operations. Let them know when you are harassed. Since the FBI and police thrive on secrecy, public exposure can undermine their ability to subvert our work.

7. Don't try to tough it out alone. Don't let others fret and suffer by themselves. Make sure that activists who are under extreme stress get the help they need (someone to talk with, rest, therapy, etc.). It is crucial that we build support networks and take care of one another.

8. Above all, do not let our movements be diverted from their main goals. Our most powerful weapon against political repression is effective organizing around the needs and issues which directly affect people's lives.

The specific methods of covert action which we know the FBI and police used in the 1960s are described below, under the categories of: (1) infiltration by agents and informers; (2) psychological warfare from the outside; (3) harassment through the legal system; and (4) extralegal force and violence. The following recommendations for protecting against each type of attack are meant to provide starting points for discussion. They are based on the author's 25 years of experience as an activist and lawyer, and on talks with long-time organizers from a broad range of movements. By adapting these guidelines to particular conditions and experimenting with new approaches, we can determine together how best to protect our movements and ourselves.

1. Infiltration by Agents and Informers

Infiltrators are agents (law enforcement officers disguised as activists) or informers (non-agents, often paid by the government) who work in a movement or community under the direction of a law enforcement or intelligence agency. Informers may be recruited from within a group or sent in by an agency, or they may be disaffected former members or supporters. They are generally untrained and hard for the agency to control.

In the past, the FBI had to rely mainly on informers or local police infiltrators because it had very few Black, Latin, or female agents, and its strict dress and grooming code left white male agents unable to look like activists. As a modern "equal opportunity employer," today's FBI has fewer such limitations. (As of 1988, however, its agents were still only 4 percent Black, 4 percent Hispanic, and 9 percent female, and members of all three groups had sued the Bureau because of employment discrimination.[99])

COINTELPRO documents and the confessions of former agents and informers indicate that while some 1960s infiltrators operated under "deep cover," discreetly spying for years without calling attention to themselves, others functioned as *provocateurs*. These operatives were directed to "seize every opportunity to carry out disruptive activity not only at meetings, conventions, etc., but also during social and other contacts."[100] They spread rumors and made unfounded accusations to inflame disagreements among activists and provoke splits. They urged divisive proposals, sabotaged important activities, squandered scarce resources, stole funds, seduced leaders, exacerbated rivalries, provoked jealousy, and publicly embarrassed progressive groups. They repeatedly led zealous activists into unnecessary danger and set them up for prosecution.[101]

While individual agents and informers advanced COINTELPRO objectives in these myriad ways, their very presence served a crucial strategic function: it promoted a paranoia that undermined trust among activists and scared off potential supporters. This effect was enhanced by covertly spread rumors exaggerating the extent to which a particular movement or group was infiltrated. As one close student of the FBI has observed:

It is not the information furnished by the spy that makes him a prized Bureau asset but the fact that he is there: a concealed hostile presence to instill fear…

It is this…that accounts for the curious dualism in American infiltration practice: while the identity of the individual informer is concealed, the fact that there is a widespread network of informers in the American left is widely publicized.[102]

The FBI often took advantage of the fear and distrust generated by this publicity to have its infiltrators claim that a dedicated activist was a government agent. This maneuver—known as placing a "snitch jacket" or "bad jacket" on an activist—serves to undermine the victim's effectiveness and to draw attention away from the actual agent. It generates confusion, fuels distrust and paranoia, diverts time and energy from a group's political work, turns co-workers against one another, and has provoked expulsions and violence.

Under COINTELPRO, snitch jackets were created in many ways. Anti-war activist Tom Hayden was jacketed through a carefully orchestrated series of news releases and newspaper articles prepared by the FBI and "cooperative" reporters.[103] Black Panther leader Huey Newton was falsely labelled an informer in FBI-composed anonymous letters supposedly from fellow prisoners in California.[104] In other operations, the FBI arranged for police to release one member of a group that had been arrested together or to single one out for special treatment, and then spread the rumor that the beneficiary had cooperated.[105] The Senate Intelligence Committee uncovered a particularly creative method:

> In another case, a local police officer was used to "jacket" the head of the Student Mobilization Committee at the University of South Carolina. The police officer picked up two members of the Committee on the pretext of interviewing them concerning narcotics. By pre-arranged signal, he had his radio operator call him with the message "[name of target] just called. Wants you to contact her. Said you have her number."[106]

The simplest and most widely used snitch jacket technique consists of planting fabricated evidence which implicates the target. The classic version of this approach is portrayed in the movie "Matewan," where the actual labor spy shows striking miners a bogus letter addressed to the union organizer on the letterhead of the company's detective agency. A more sophisticated modern variant relies on forged reports from the target to a government agency. This method was employed in 1968 against SNCC leader Stokely Carmichael (Kwame Toure), along with a "whispering campaign," to "tag Carmichael with a CIA label."[107]

The modern method proved especially effective against a top national official of the Communist Party-USA, William Albertson. In 1964, the Bureau simulated Albertson's handwriting and prepared a bogus informer's report from him to his supposed controlling agent. An FBI infiltrator then planted the bogus report in a car in which Albertson had recently been a passenger. When experts insisted that the writing was his, Albertson was expelled from the Party in disgrace.[108]

Guidelines for Coping with Infiltration

1. Be careful to avoid pushing a new or hesitant member, or one facing personal, financial, or legal problems, to take risks beyond what that person is ready to handle, particularly in situations which could result in arrest and prosecution. People in positions of legal or other jeopardy have proven especially vulnerable to recruitment as informers.

2. Deal openly with the form and content of what anyone says and does, whether the person is a suspected agent, has emotional problems, or is simply a sincere but naive or confused person new to the work.

3. Establish a process through which anyone who suspects an infiltrator (or other covert intervention) can express his or her fears without scaring others. Experienced people assigned this responsibility can do a great deal to help a group maintain its morale and focus while, at the same time, consolidating information and deciding how to use it. This plan works best when accompanied by group discussion of the danger of paranoia, so that everyone understands the reasons for following the established procedure.

4. Take steps to alert other activists any time an agent or informer admits their role or you have a concrete and verified basis for certain knowledge. (Make sure you have not been taken in by a snitch jacket.) Act immediately and use every available means, including photographs, aliases, identifying traits, and a description of methods of operation. In the 1960s, some agents managed, even after their exposure in one community, to move on and repeat their performance in others.

5. Be very cautious in attempting to expose a suspected, but unadmitted, agent or informer. The best approach depends on the nature of your group. A close-knit, self-selecting group of experienced activists, especially one which contemplates illegal activity, should exclude anyone who is not fully trusted by everyone involved. If the stakes are high, don't be afraid to trust your intuition.

An open, public organization trying to reach out and involve new people faces a very different situation. Here, an attempted exposure carries enormous risks. The suspect may claim to be the victim of discrimination and may falsely finger his or her accusers as agents. In the process, activists may be turned against one another and lose the mutual trust and respect which is vital to any successful organization. New members and potential recruits may be scared away. The group's attention and energy may be so diverted that it is no longer able to move effectively toward its main goals.

Activists who suspect infiltration of a public political organization should carefully evaluate alternatives to attempted exposure. The appropriate response depends on the kind of agent or informer you think you are dealing with.

A suspect who seems to play a passive, or even a constructive role may secretly be undermining a group's work or passing information to the FBI and police. In this situation, it often is most productive to discreetly limit the suspect's opportunities without making your suspicions public. Take steps to deny access to organizational funds, financial records, mailing lists, office equipment, planning and security committees, discussions of illegal activity, and meetings that plan criminal defense strategy. Go public if you later catch the person in the act (but not merely with incriminating evidence which could have been planted or forged).

A different approach is required if the suspect is an active disrupter or *provocateur*. In this case, it is most constructive to confront the form and content of what the suspect says and does, without making an issue of why he or she says or does it. Start with a discreet private talk, since the suspect could be merely naive or misguided. If the harmful behavior persists, you probably will have to take it on in an open group discussion. Plan in advance how to limit the risk of disruption and demoralization. If you need to exclude or expel the suspect, be sure to inform other activists of your decision and reasons.

2. Psychological Warfare From the Outside

While boring from within, the FBI and police also attack dissident movements from the outside. They openly mount propaganda campaigns through public addresses, news releases, books, pamphlets, magazine articles, radio, and television. They also use covert deception and manipulation. Documented tactics of this kind include:

False Media Stories: COINTELPRO documents expose frequent collusion between news media personnel and the FBI to publish false and distorted material at the Bureau's behest. The FBI routinely leaked derogatory information to its collaborators in the news media. It also created newspaper and magazine articles and television "documentaries" which the media knowingly or unknowingly carried as their own. Copies were sent anonymously or under bogus letterhead to activists' financial backers, employers, business associates, families, neighbors, church officials, school administrators, landlords, and whomever else might cause them trouble.[109]

One FBI media fabrication claimed that Jean Seberg, a white film star active in anti-racist causes, was pregnant by a prominent Black leader. The Bureau leaked the story anonymously to columnist Joyce

Haber and also had it passed to her by a "friendly" source in the *Los Angeles Times* editorial staff. The item appeared without attribution in Haber's nationally syndicated column of May 19, 1970. Seberg's husband has sued the FBI as responsible for her resulting stillbirth, nervous breakdown, and suicide.[110]

Bogus Leaflets, Pamphlets, and Other Publications: COIN-TELPRO documents show that the FBI routinely put out phony leaflets, posters, pamphlets, newspapers, and other publications in the name of movement groups. The purpose was to discredit the groups and turn them against one another.

FBI cartoon leaflets were used to divide and disrupt the main national anti-war coalition of the late 1960s. Similar fliers were circulated in 1968 and 1969 in the name of the Black Panthers and the United Slaves (US), a rival Black nationalist group based in Southern California. The phony Panther/US leaflets, together with other covert operations, were credited with subverting a fragile truce between the two groups and igniting an explosion of internecine violence that left four Panthers dead, many more wounded, and a once-flourishing regional Black movement decimated.[111]

Another major COINTELPRO operation involved a children's coloring book which the Black Panther Party had rejected as anti-white and gratuitously violent. The FBI revised the coloring book to make it even more offensive. Its field offices then distributed thousands of copies anonymously or under phony organizational letterheads. Many backers of the Party's program of free breakfasts for children withdrew their support after the FBI conned them into believing that the bogus coloring book was being used in the program.[112]

Forged Correspondence: Former employees have confirmed that the FBI has the capacity to produce state-of-the-art forgery.[113] This capacity was used under COINTELPRO to create snitch jackets and bogus communications that exacerbated differences among activists and disrupted their work.

One such forgery intimidated civil rights worker Muhammed Kenyatta (Donald Jackson), causing him to abandon promising projects in Jackson, Mississippi. Kenyatta had foundation grants to form Black economic cooperatives and open a "Black and Proud School" for dropouts. He was also a student organizer at nearby Tougaloo College. In the winter of 1969, after an extended campaign of FBI and police harassment, Kenyatta received a letter, purportedly from the Tougaloo College Defense Committee, which "directed" that he cease his political activities immediately. If he did not "heed our diplomatic and well-thought-out warning," the committee would consider taking measures

A key 1960s covert operation that fueled antagonism between emerging tendencies among progressive women did not come to light until almost 20 years later. When women speakers at the national counter-inaugural rally in 1969 raised issues of women's oppression, men in the audience had shouted them down and threatened sexual violence. Shaken by the incident, women activists met at the home of one of the speakers, Marilyn Webb, to analyze what had happened and decide whether to keep trying to work within the New Left. As they talked, the phone rang and a woman's voice threatened Webb: "If you or anybody else like you ever gives a speech like that again, we're going to beat the shit out of you. SDS has a line on women's liberation, and that is *the line.*"

The voice and content of the call made it appear to be from Cathy Wilkerson, a well-known SDS organizer who was in the same women's group as many of the women in the room. The women assumed that Wilkerson had, in fact, made the call, and the story spread across the country, provoking bitter anger. It was only at an SDS reunion in the summer of 1988, that Webb learned that neither Wilkerson nor any other SDS woman had made such a call.[114]

"which would have a more direct effect and which would not be as cordial as this note." Kenyatta and his wife left. Only years later did they learn it was not Tougaloo students, but FBI covert operators who had driven them out.[115]

Later in 1969, FBI agents fabricated a letter to the mainly white organizers of a proposed Washington, D.C. anti-war rally demanding that they pay the local Black community a $20,000 "security bond." This attempted extortion was composed in the name of the local Black United Front (BUF) and signed with the forged signature of its leader. FBI informers inside the BUF then tried to get the group to back such a demand, and Bureau contacts in the media made sure the story received wide publicity.[116]

The Senate Intelligence Committee uncovered a series of FBI letters sent to top Panther leaders throughout 1970 in the name of Connie Mathews, an intermediary between the Black Panther Party's national office and Panther leader Eldridge Cleaver, in exile in Algeria. These exquisite forgeries were prepared on pilfered stationery in Panther vernacular expertly simulated by the FBI's Washington, D.C. laboratory. Each was forwarded to an FBI Legal Attaché at a U.S. Embassy in a foreign country that Mathews was due to travel through and then posted at just the right time "in such a manner that it cannot be traced to the Bureau."

The FBI enhanced the eerie authenticity of these fabrications by lacing them with esoteric personal tidbits culled from electronic surveillance of Panther homes and offices. Combined with other forgeries, anonymous letters and phone calls, and the covert intervention of FBI and police infiltrators, the Mathews correspondence succeeded in inflaming intra-party mistrust and rivalry until it erupted into the bitter public split that shattered the organization in the winter of 1971.[117]

Anonymous Letters and Telephone Calls: During the 1960s, activists received a steady flow of anonymous letters and phone calls which turn out to have been from the FBI. Some were unsigned, while others bore bogus names or purported to come from unidentified activists in phony or actual organizations.[118]

Many of these bogus communications promoted racial divisions and fears, often by exploiting and exacerbating tensions between Jewish and Black activists. One such FBI-concocted letter went to SDS members who had joined Black students protesting New York University's discharge of a Black teacher in 1969. The supposed author, an unnamed "SDS member," urged whites to break ranks and abandon the Black students because of alleged anti-Semitic slurs by the fired teacher and his supporters.[119]

Other anonymous letters and phone calls falsely accused movement leaders of collaboration with the authorities, corruption, or sexual affairs with other activists' mates. The letter on the next page was used to provoke "a lasting distrust" between a Black civil rights leader and his wife. Its FBI authors hoped that his "concern over what to do about it" would "detract from his time spent in the plots and plans of his organization."[120] As in the Seberg incident, inter-racial sex was a persistent theme. The husband of one white woman active in civil rights and anti-war work filed for divorce soon after receiving the FBI-authored letter reproduced on page 50.

Still other anonymous FBI communications were designed to intimidate dissidents, disrupt coalitions, and provoke violence. Calls to Stokely Carmichael's mother warning of a fictitious Black Panther murder plot drove him to leave the country in September 1968.[121] Similar anonymous FBI telephone threats to SNCC leader James Forman were instrumental in thwarting efforts to bring the two groups together.[122]

The Chicago FBI made effective use of anonymous letters to sabotage the Panthers efforts to build alliances with previously apolitical Black street gangs. The most extensive of these operations involved the Black P. Stone Nation, or "Blackstone Rangers," a powerful confederation of several thousand local Black youth. Early in 1969, as FBI and police infiltrators in the Rangers spread rumors of an impending Panther

FBI anonymous letter to disrupt marriage and political activity of Black community leader.

attack, the Bureau sent Ranger chief Jeff Fort an incendiary note signed "a black brother you don't know." Fort's supposed friend warned that "The brothers that run the Panthers blame you for blocking their thing and there's supposed to be a hit out for you."[123] Another FBI-concocted anonymous "black man" then informed Chicago Panther leader Fred Hampton of a Ranger plot "to get you out of the way." These fabrications squelched promising talks between the two groups and enabled Chicago Panther security chief William O'Neal, an FBI-paid *provocateur,* to instigate a series of armed confrontations from which the Panthers barely managed to escape without serious casualties.[124]

Pressure Through Employers, Landlords, and Others: FBI records reveal repeated maneuvers to generate pressure on dissidents from their parents, children, spouses, landlords, employers, college administrators, church superiors, welfare agencies, credit bureaus, and the like. Anonymous letters and telephone calls were often used to this end. Confidential official communications were effective in bringing to bear the Bureau's immense power and authority.[125]

Agents' reports indicate that such FBI intervention denied Martin Luther King, Jr., and other 1960s activists any number of foundation grants and public speaking engagements.[126] It also deprived alternative newspapers of their printers, suppliers, and distributors and cost them crucial advertising revenues when major record companies were persuaded to take their business elsewhere.[127] Similar government manipulation may underlie steps recently taken by some insurance companies to cancel policies held by churches giving sanctuary to refugees from El Salvador and Guatemala.

Tampering With Mail and Telephone Service: The FBI and CIA routinely used mail covers (the recording of names and addresses) and electronic surveillance in order to spy on 1960s movements. The CIA alone admitted to photographing the outside of 2.7 million pieces of first-class mail during the 1960s and to opening almost 215,000. Government agencies also tampered with mail, altering, delaying, or "disappearing" it. Activists were quick to blame one another, and infiltrators easily exploited the situation to exacerbate their tensions.[128]

FBI anonymous letter to undermine a white woman activist's civil rights and anti-war work.

FBI Fronts

COINTELPRO documents reveal that a number of 1960s political groups and projects were actually set up and operated by the FBI.[129] One, "Grupo pro-Uso Voto del MPI," was used to disrupt the fragile unity developing in the mid-1960s among the MPI (Movimiento Pro Independencia, forerunner of the Puerto Rican Socialist Party) and other groups seeking Puerto Rico's independence from the United States. The genuine proponents of independence had joined together around a common strategy of boycotting colonial elections which the U.S. government manipulated (through its control of the island's economy, media, schools, and police) to legitimize continued U.S. rule. The bogus group, pretending to support independence, urged independentistas to ignore the boycott and go to the polls.[130]

Since FBI front groups are basically a means for penetrating and disrupting dissident movements, it is best to deal with them on the basis of the Guidelines for Coping with Infiltration. Confront what a suspect group says and does, but avoid public accusations unless you have definite proof. If you do have such proof, share it with everyone affected.

Dissidents' telephone communications often were similarly obstructed. The SDS Regional Office in Washington, D.C., for instance, mysteriously lost its phone service the week preceding virtually every national anti-war demonstration in the late 1960s.[131]

Disinformation to Prevent or Disrupt Movement Meetings and Activities: A favorite COINTELPRO tactic uncovered by Senate investigators was to advertise a non-existent political event, or to misinform people of the time and place of an actual one. They reported a variety of disruptive FBI "dirty tricks" designed to cast blame on the organizers of movement events.

In one "disinformation" case, the [FBI's] Chicago Field Office duplicated blank forms prepared by the National Mobilization Committee to End the War in Vietnam ("NMC") soliciting housing for demonstrators at the Democratic National Convention. Chicago filled out 217 of these forms with fictitious names and addresses and sent them to the NMC, which provided them to demonstrators who made "long and useless journeys to locate these addresses." The NMC then decided to discard all replies received on the housing forms rather than have out-of-town demonstrators try to locate nonexistent addresses. (The same program was carried out when the Washington Mobilization Committee distributed housing forms for demonstrators coming to Washington for the 1969 Presidential inaugural ceremonies.)

In another case, during the demonstrations accompanying in-auguration ceremonies, the Washington Field Office discovered that NMC marshals were using walkie-talkies to coordinate their move-ments and activities. WFO used the same citizen band to supply the marshals with misinformation and, pretending to be an NMC unit, countermanded NMC orders.

In a third case, a [Bureau] midwest field office disrupted arrange-ments for state university students to attend the 1969 inaugural demonstrations by making a series of anonymous telephone calls to the transportation company. The calls were designed to confuse both the transportation company and the SDS leaders as to the cost of transportation and the time and place for leaving and returning. This office also placed confusing leaflets around the campus to show different times and places for demonstration-planning meetings, as well as conflicting times and dates for traveling to Washington.[132]

Guidelines for Coping with Psychological Warfare

1. Verify and double-check all arrangements for housing, transpor-tation, meeting rooms, and so forth. Don't assume movement organizers are at fault if something goes wrong.

2. Don't believe everything you hear or read. Check with the supposed source of the information before acting on it. Use a neutral third party if necessary. Personal communication among estranged activists, however difficult or painful, could have countered many FBI operations which proved effective in the 1960s.

3. When you discover bogus materials, false media stories, or forged documents, publicly disavow them and expose the true source, insofar as you can.

4. When you hear a negative, confusing, or potentially harmful rumor, don't pass it on. Instead, discuss it with a trusted friend or with the people in your group who are responsible for dealing with such matters.

5. Don't gossip about personal tensions, rivalries, and disagree-ments. This just feeds and amplifies rumors. Moreover, if you gossip where you can be overheard, you may add to the pool of information that the FBI and police use to divide our movements. (Note that the CIA has the technology to read mail without opening it and that telephones, including pay phones, can be tapped by a computer programmed to record conversations in which specified words appear.)[133]

6. Be sure to make time in group meetings for open, honest discussion and resolution of "personal" as well as "political" issues. This is the best way to reduce tensions and hostilities and the urge to gossip about them.

7. Warn your parents, friends, neighbors, and others who may be contacted by government agents. Consider telling them what you are doing and why before they hear the FBI's version. Provide them with materials which explain their legal rights and the dangers of talking with the FBI. Offer to connect them with lawyers and support groups.

3. Harassment Through the Legal System

Assigned official responsibility for investigating crimes, the FBI and police abuse their authority in order to attack radical activists. In the guise of law enforcement, they used a range of tactics to discredit and disrupt 1960s movements.

Conspicuous Surveillance: The FBI and police blatantly watched activists' homes, followed their cars, opened their mail, and attended their political events. The object was not to collect information (which is done surreptitiously), but to harass and intimidate.[134]

"Investigative" Interviews: FBI agents often extracted damaging information from activists who did not know their legal right to refuse to speak or who thought they could outsmart the FBI. But the purpose of supposedly investigative interviews was actually far broader. They provided a powerful means of intimidation, scaring off potential activists and driving away those who had already become involved. Orchestrated campaigns of interviews were used to create a climate of fear among dissidents and their supporters. COINTELPRO directives advised widespread interviewing of activists and their friends, relatives, and associates to "enhance the paranoia endemic in these circles" and "get the point across that there is an FBI agent behind every mailbox."[135]

Grand Juries: Unlike an FBI request to talk, a grand jury subpoena carries legal penalties for non-cooperation. Those who refuse to testify, despite immunity from direct use of that testimony against them, can be jailed for contempt of court and may face criminal charges. (Such limited immunity still allows use of a witness's testimony against other activists and even to obtain other evidence against the testifying witness. It enables prosecutors to get around the Fifth Amendment right against compulsory self-incrimination.)

This process has been manipulated to turn the grand jury into an instrument of political repression. Frustrated by the consistent refusal of trial juries to convict on charges of overtly political crimes, the FBI and the U.S. Justice Department convened over 100 grand juries in the late 1960s and subpoenaed more than 1,000 activists from the Black, Puerto Rican, student, women's, and anti-war movements.[136] Pursuit of fugitives and alleged terrorists was the usual pretext. Many targets were so terrified

that they dropped out of political activity. Others were jailed for contempt of court without any criminal charge or trial. This use of the contempt power is a scaled-down version of the political internment employed in South Africa and Northern Ireland.

Discriminatory Enforcement of Tax Laws and Other Government Regulations: The FBI arranged for special, meticulous audits of tax returns filed by dissident activists and organizations. It worked with the Internal Revenue Service to deny or revoke the tax-exempt status of educational, charitable, and religious organizations that lawfully aided progressive causes.[137]

The FBI and police similarly arranged for local authorities to selectively enforce building codes, health regulations, and zoning laws in order to fine or shut down alternative institutions such as child care centers, medical clinics, and the GI coffeehouses that movement groups ran near major U.S. military bases. They wreaked havoc with the licenses of progressive lawyers, doctors, and other professionals. When 1960s activists had to show identification (e.g., upon entering a courtroom to witness a political trial), they could expect to be jailed if they had left parking tickets or other minor fines unpaid.[138]

False Arrest: COINTELPRO directives cite as exemplary the Philadelphia FBI's 1967 success in having local militants "arrested on every possible charge until they could no longer make bail" and "spent most of the summer in jail."[139] FBI agents across the country were advised that since the "purpose…is to disrupt…it is immaterial whether facts exist to substantiate the charge."[140] Accordingly, activists were repeatedly arrested on flimsy charges which were dropped long before trial.

This technique was particularly effective in disrupting movement activities. Street sellers of underground newspapers were routinely rounded up when their paper was about to come out.[141] In one case, Chicago Panther leader Fred Hampton was arrested in a local television studio as he was about to appear on a popular talk show, and then released when the program ended.[142] The Black Panthers were hit with 768 arrests between May 1967 and December 1969 alone.[143]

Political Trials: While many of the 1960s activists who were rounded up in this manner were quickly released, others faced full-blown prosecution. Among those tried for alleged crimes were: Dr. Benjamin Spock, Rev. William Sloane Coffin, and other advocates and organizers of draft resistance; Fathers Daniel and Phillip Berrigan and their Catholic pacifist compatriots; leaders of the 1968 Democratic Party Convention protests (the "Chicago 8 Conspiracy Trial"); national SNCC chair H. Rap Brown; and prominent Black communist professor and activist Angela Davis.[144] By the summer of 1969, the surviving non-imprisoned and non-exiled national officers of the Black Panther Party were on trial, along with the leaders of key Panther chapters in New York City, Los Angeles, and New Haven.[145]

In case after case, the government's political motives, fabricated evidence, and perjured testimony were exposed and the defendants were acquitted by jurors profoundly moved by the trial experience. In the process, however, the 1960s movements suffered enormously. The trials achieved the effect that the FBI secretly intended: to "exhaust and demoralize" dissident movements, "even if actual prosecution is not successful as far as convictions are concerned."[146]

In most cases, the initial horrifying criminal charges (such as an alleged Panther plot to bomb crowded New York City department stores) received far more publicity than the eventual acquittals. The cost of lawyers, investigators, transcripts, depositions, expert witnesses, and other requisites of effective criminal defense proved staggering. Millions of dollars more had to be raised for bail bonds, a reported $4,890,580 by the Panthers alone during the period between May 1967 and December 1969.[147] Those defendants who could not make bail, mainly Blacks and Latinos, were removed from their communities and jailed for months and even years. Though political trials sometimes provided a useful focus for public education, their main effect was to slander progressive movements, drain their resources, and cause activists to "burn out" in defensive efforts that left little time or energy for organizing around issues which affect ordinary people's lives.

Wrongful Imprisonment: Though most 1960s activists tried on political charges were eventually acquitted, many were convicted and imprisoned. Some were simply framed, such as Black anarchist Martin Sostre, sentenced to 30 to 41 years for allegedly selling narcotics from his radical bookstore in Buffalo, New York.[148] Others, including Black Panther founder Huey Newton and Cleveland Black militant Ahmed Evans, were lured into armed self-defense for which they (but not their assailants) were convicted after rigged trials.[149]

Still other 1960s activists were victims of the selective enforcement of laws routinely ignored throughout U.S. society. Lee Otis Johnson, a SNCC organizer in Texas, received a 30-year sentence for allegedly passing a single joint of marijuana to an undercover agent.[150] John Sinclair, leader of Detroit's White Panther Party and editor of several alternative newspapers, was sentenced to ten years in a maximum security prison for possessing two joints.[151]

·Years later, the trials of imprisoned COINTELPRO targets were reviewed by the world human rights organization Amnesty International. Amnesty found official abuse to be so pervasive and egregious in these cases as to cast serious doubt on all the resulting convictions. It called for an official "commission of inquiry into the effect of domestic intelligence activities on criminal trials in the United States of America."[152]

Manipulation of Probation and Parole: Particularly vulnerable were 1960s activists with pre-movement criminal records. Outspoken revolutionary prisoners such as George Jackson were repeatedly turned down by parole boards that had long since released inmates with comparable records.[153] Eldridge Cleaver, national Panther official and 1968 U.S. presidential candidate of the Peace and Freedom Party, had his parole revoked because of criminal charges stemming from an April 1968 incident in which a group of Panthers were ambushed by Oakland, California police.[154] Cleaver's consequent exile, fearing he would be murdered in prison, set the stage for the COINTELPRO operations that eventually shattered the party.

Guidelines for Coping with Harassment Through the Legal System

1. Don't talk to the FBI, and don't let them in without a warrant. Keep careful records of what they say and do. Tell others that they came. (For more detailed advice and information, see the box on page 58.)

2. If an activist does talk, or makes some other honest error, explain the serious harm that could result. Be firm, but do not ostracize a sincere person who slips up. Isolation only weakens a person's ability to resist. It can drive someone out of the movement and even into the hands of the police.

3. If FBI or other government agents start to harass people in your area, alert everyone to refuse to cooperate. Warn your friends, neighbors, parents, children, and anyone else who might be contacted. Make sure people know what to do and where to call for help. Get literature, films, and other materials through the organizations listed in the back of this book. Set up community meetings with speakers who have resisted similar harassment elsewhere. Contact sympathetic reporters. Consider "Wanted" posters with photos of the agents, or guerrilla theater which follows them through the city streets.

4. Organizations listed in the back can also help resist grand jury harassment. Community education is important, along with child care and legal, financial, and other support for those who protect a movement by refusing to divulge information. If a respected activist is subpoenaed for obviously political reasons, consider trying to arrange for sanctuary in a local church or synagogue.

If the FBI Drops By, *JUST SAY NO!*

1. You do not have to talk to FBI agents, police, or other investigators. You do not have to talk to them in your house, on the street, if you've been arrested, or even in jail. Only a court or grand jury has legal authority to compel testimony.

2. You don't have to let the FBI or police into your home or office unless they show you an arrest or search warrant which authorizes them to enter that specific place.

3. If they do present a warrant, you do not have to tell them anything other than your name and address. You have a right to observe what they do. Make written notes, including the agents' names, agency, and badge numbers. Try to have other people present as witnesses, and have them make written notes too.

4. Anything you say to an FBI agent or other law enforcement officer may be used against you and other people.

5. Giving the FBI or police information may mean that you will have to testify to the same information at a trial or before a grand jury.

6. Lying to an FBI agent or other federal investigator is a crime.

7. The best advice, if the FBI or police try to question you or to enter your home or office without a warrant, is to JUST SAY NO. FBI agents have a job to do, and they are highly skilled at it. Attempting to outwit them is very risky. *You can never tell how a seemingly harmless bit of information can help them hurt you or someone else.*

8. The FBI or police may threaten you with a grand jury subpoena if you don't give them information. But you may get one anyway, and anything you've already told them will be the basis for more detailed questioning under oath. (If you do get a subpoena, you might be able to fight it with help from groups listed on page 92.)

9. They may try to threaten or intimidate you by pretending to have information about you: "We know what you have been doing, but if you cooperate it will be all right." If you are concerned about this, tell them you will talk to them with your lawyer present.

10. If you are nervous about simply refusing to talk, you may find it easier to tell them to contact your lawyer. Once a lawyer is involved, the FBI and police usually pull back since they have lost their power to intimidate. (Make arrangements with sympathetic local lawyers and let everyone know that agents who visit them can be referred to these lawyers. Organizations listed on page 92 can help locate lawyers.)

5. If your group engages in civil disobedience or finds itself under intense police pressure, start a bail fund, train some members to deal with the legal system, and develop an ongoing relationship with sympathetic local lawyers.

6. If you anticipate arrest, do not carry address books or any other materials which could help the FBI and police.

7. While the FBI and police are entirely capable of fabricating criminal charges, your non-political law violations make it easier for them to set you up. Be careful with drugs, tax returns, traffic tickets, and so forth. The point is not to get paranoid, but to make a realistic assessment based on your visibility and other relevant circumstances.

8. When an activist has to appear in court, make sure he or she is not alone. The presence of supporters is crucial for morale and can help influence jurors.

9. Don't neglect jailed activists. Organize visits, correspondence, books, food packages, child care, etc. Keep publicizing their cases.

10. Publicize FBI and police abuses through sympathetic journalists and your own media (posters, leaflets, public access cable television, etc.). Don't let the government and corporate media be the only ones to shape public perceptions of FBI and police attacks on political activists.

In Berkeley, California in the late 1960s, activists used whistles, noisemakers, and spotlights to ward off FBI and police harassment. When law enforcement personnel entered an area, the first person to spot them would alert other activists in the vicinity. Soon dozens of people were gathered around the intruders, blowing loud whistles, shining bright lights on them, and demanding that they leave. The effect was to ridicule the FBI and police and undermine their intimidating mystique. Activists had fun in the process, and gained a sense of their collective power.

---

4. Extralegal Force and Violence

A late 1960s COINTELPRO communique urged that "The Negro youth and moderates must be made to understand that if they succumb to revolutionary teaching, they will be dead revolutionaries."[155] In this spirit, the FBI and police created a virtual reign of terror in movement communities. Their methods included:

Government Instigation of "Private" Violence: FBI records reveal covert maneuvers to get the Mafia to move against Black activist-comedian Dick Gregory and the entire leadership of the Communist Party-USA ("Operation Hoodwink").[156] The Bureau also used infiltrators, forgeries, and anonymous notes and telephone calls to incite violent rivals to attack Malcolm X, the Black Panther Party, and other targets. One COINTELPRO report boasted that "shootings, beatings and a high degree of unrest continue to prevail in the ghetto area...it is felt that a substantial amount of the unrest is directly attributable to this program."[157]

To goad the right-wing Jewish Defense League (JDL) into attacking the Panthers, the New York FBI invented a Black World War II veteran who wrote anonymously to JDL head Rabbi Meir Kahane. The FBI "GI" told Kahane a heart-rending story of how he came to respect Jews when "a Jewish Army Dr. named Rothstein" saved his life and a Jewish teacher, "Mr. Katz," helped him in school. He complained that his oldest son had started calling him "a Jew boy's slave" after joining the Panthers. In a progression of letters, Kahane's phony pen pal warned more and more urgently of Panther plans to extort money from Jewish merchants and bomb Jewish stores. The FBI then sat back and watched Blacks and Jews slug it out on the streets of Harlem, confirming each group's worst fears.[158]

Covert Government Aid to Right-Wing Vigilantes: In the guise of using COINTELPRO against "white hate groups," the FBI actually subsidized, armed, directed, and protected a sordid array of racist, right-wing thugs. One such group, a "Secret Army Organization" of California ex-Minutemen led by FBI operative Howard Godfrey, beat up Chicano activists, tore apart the offices of the San Diego *Street Journal* and the Movement for a Democratic Military, and tried to kill a prominent anti-war organizer.[159] Defectors from the Legion of Justice, a Chicago-based vigilante band that wrecked movement bookstores, newspaper offices, and film studios, testified that they had been secretly armed and financed by the U.S. Army's 113th Military Intelligence Group and that their targets had been selected by the Chicago Police Department red squad.[160]

The FBI's main right-wing beneficiary was the Ku Klux Klan. In 1961, the FBI supplied the advance information that enabled the Klan to brutalize freedom riders as they arrived in various Southern cities. FBI operative Gary Thomas Rowe shot one of the guns when the KKK murdered civil rights worker Viola Liuzo in 1963. He helped plan the bombing that took the lives of four Black children at a Birmingham, Alabama, church that same year. By 1965, some 20 percent of Klan members were on the FBI payroll. Many occupied positions of power: "FBI agents reached leadership positions in seven of the fourteen Klan groups across the country, headed one state Klan organization and even created a splinter Klan group which grew to nearly two hundred members."[161]

Government Burglaries and Vandalism: Former agents confessed to thousands of "black bag jobs" in which the FBI broke into dissidents' offices, homes, and cars. Some of these burglaries were carried out stealthily, to copy records, steal papers, sabotage machinery, or plant bugs, drugs, or guns, without the targets' knowledge. In one operation, FBI agents broke in to steal the personal diary of a member of the Progressive Labor Party, forged entries to set up a snitch jacket, and then broke in again to plant the incriminating evidence.[162]

Many other bag jobs were blatantly crude, designed to intimidate activists and their supporters. Government infiltrators later admitted numerous other acts of vandalism, ranging from broken windows to fire-bombings.[163] Late 1960s FBI and police raids laid waste to underground press offices across the country.[164] Historian Robert Goldstein has provided an account of similar raids on the offices of the Black Panther Party:

> From April to December 1969, police raided Panther headquarters in San Francisco, Chicago, Salt Lake City, Indianapolis, Denver, San Diego, Sacramento and Los Angeles, including four separate raids in Chicago, two in San Diego and two in Los Angeles...

Police raids frequently involved severe damage to Panther head-quarters. Thus, during a raid at Sacramento in June, 1969, in search of an alleged sniper who was never found, police sprayed the building with tear gas, shot up the walls, broke typewriters and destroyed bulk food which the Panthers were distributing free to ghetto children...During raids on Panther headquarters in Philadelphia in September, 1970, police ransacked the office, ripped out plumbing and chopped up and carted away furniture. Six Panthers were led into the street, placed against a wall and stripped as Police Chief Frank Rizzo boasted to newsmen, "Imagine the big Black Panthers with their pants down."[165]

Government Assaults, Beatings, and Killings: Under the guise of enforcing the law, FBI agents and police officers routinely roughed up 1960s activists and often threatened or injured them. The coordinator of the PEN American Center's Freedom to Write Committee recorded the experience of one alternative newspaper:

> *Kudzu*, produced in Jackson, Mississippi, served as a major organiza-tional center for the New Left and counterculture in that area. The tenacity of the paper and its allies can be gauged by the fact that by 1968 the newspaper had survived a conviction on obscenity charges, the arrest of salespeople, the confiscation of cameras, and even eviction from its offices. On October 8, 1968, eighteen staff members and supporters of *Kudzu* were attacked and beaten by Jackson deputy sheriffs...In 1970, *Kudzu* was put under direct surveillance by the FBI. For more than two months FBI agents made daily searches without warrants...On October 24 and 25, *Kudzu* sponsored a Southern regional conference of the Underground Press Syndicate. The night before the conference the FBI and Jackson detectives searched the *Kudzu* offices twice. During the search, an FBI agent threatened to kill *Kudzu* staffers. On the morning of October 26, FBI agents again searched the offices. That evening local police entered the building, held its eight occupants at gunpoint, produced a bag of marijuana, then arrested them...A *Kudzu* staff member commented, "The FBI used to be fairly sophisticated, but lately they have broken one of our doors, pointed guns in our faces, told us that 'punks like you don't have any rights,' and threatened to shoot us on the street if they see us with our hands in our pockets."[166]

Similar violence was used to disperse 1960s demonstrations, with provocative acts by undercover agents often providing a convenient pretext. Southern police attacks on civil rights workers in the early 1960s have been widely publicized, most recently in the documentary film "Eyes on the Prize." Contrary to the impression promoted by the media, however, 1960s police brutality against political protesters was not limited to any one period or region. As progressive momentum surged in the final years of the decade, "Southern justice" spread throughout the country. Unarmed demonstrators were attacked by police and national guardsmen in Ohio (Kent State), Kansas, Wisconsin, Illinois, New York, California, and Puerto Rico as well as Mississippi (Jackson State) and North Carolina (Orangeburg). Thousands were beaten and injured. Hundreds were wounded and hospitalized. At least 17 were killed.[167]

Political Assassination: While activists from all walks of life were randomly beaten and killed by police and guardsmen, Black leaders targeted under COINTELPRO faced "neutralization" through premeditated murder. In Houston, Texas, in July 1970, police assassinated Carl Hampton, Black leader of that city's burgeoning Peoples Party.[168] In Oakland, California, in April 1968, Bobby Hutton, national finance minister of the Black Panther Party, was gunned down as he emerged unarmed, hands held high, from the police ambush which drove Eldridge Cleaver into exile.[169] In Chicago, in December 1969, the FBI, police, and state's attorney joined forces in the cold-blooded murder of Illinois Black Panther Party chairman Fred Hampton.[170]

The murder of Fred Hampton was especially pivotal. Hampton was a charismatic leader who developed a broad following in the Black community and organized the first multi-racial "rainbow coalition." In the late fall of 1969, he agreed to take the reins of the national party organization after its initial leaders were jailed or forced into exile. At that point, having failed in its efforts to get Hampton rubbed out by local street gangs, the FBI arranged to have the job done by a special squad of police assigned to the state's attorney's office.

The Bureau provided a detailed floorplan of Hampton's home marked to show where Hampton slept. Its paid informer, William O'Neal, Hampton's personal bodyguard, drugged Hampton's Kool-Aid so he would remain unconscious through the night. As the Panthers slept, O'Neal slipped out and a 14-man hit squad armed with automatic weapons crashed into Hampton's home and pumped in over 200 rounds of ammunition. When their fire subsided, Hampton and Mark Clark lay dead and seven other Panthers were wounded.

The incident was subsequently investigated by a blue-ribbon citizens' commission and litigated at length in the federal courts. Despite an elaborate law enforcement cover-up, Hampton's death was found to be the result not of a shootout, as claimed by the authorities, but of a carefully orchestrated, Vietnam-style "search and destroy" mission.[171] The federal and local governments had to pay $1.8 million in damages to the parents and survivors.

These thoroughly documented findings, viewed in the context of the whole history of COINTELPRO, lend credence to the widely held, enduring suspicion that the FBI or CIA were also behind the assassination of the two most important progressive U.S. leaders of the decade, Malcolm X and Martin Luther King, Jr.[172]

Guidelines for Coping with Extralegal Force and Violence:

1. Establish security procedures appropriate to your group's level of activity and discuss them thoroughly with everyone involved. Control access to keys, files, letterhead, funds, financial records, mailing lists, etc.

2. Keep duplicates of valuable documents, records, files, computer disks, etc. in a safe place separate from your home or office.

3. Remember that cars are easily broken into (especially trunks) and that trash can easily be rifled and searched.

Upon hearing of Fred Hampton's murder, the Black Panthers in Los Angeles fortified their offices and organized a communications network to alert the community and news media in the event of a raid. When the police did attempt an armed assault four days later, the Panthers were able to hold off the attack until a large community and media presence enabled them to leave the office without serious casualties.[173] Similar preparation can help other groups to deal with expected right-wing or police assaults.

---

4. Make a public issue of any form of crude harassment. Contact your congressperson. Call the media. Demonstrate at your local FBI, police, or right-wing organization's office. Turn the attack into an opportunity for explaining how domestic covert action threatens fundamental human rights.

5. Keep careful records of break-ins, thefts, bomb threats, raids, brutality, conspicuous surveillance, and other harassment. They will help you to discern patterns and to prepare reports and testimony.

6. Share this information and your experiences combatting such attacks with the Movement Support Network and other groups which document and analyze repression and resistance countrywide. (See resource groups listing in back of book.)

7. If you experience or anticipate intense harassment, develop contingency plans and an emergency telephone network so you can rapidly mobilize community support and media attention. Consider better locks, window bars, alarm systems, fireproof locked cabinets, etc.

8. Be sure that some members are well trained in first aid. Keep medical supplies up-to-date and know how to contact sympathetic doctors and nurses and get to the nearest hospital.

9. Make sure your group designates and prepares other members to step in if leaders are jailed or otherwise incapacitated. The more each participant is able to think for herself or himself and take responsibility, the greater the group's capacity to cope with crises.

• Exposing Domestic Covert Action as Undemocratic and a Form of Terrorism

To build strong movements for social justice, it is essential that activists study and discuss the methods of covert action and prepare to deal with them. Since such attacks depend on secrecy, it is also important that they be exposed to the widest possible audience. The bare facts should be sufficient to outrage most people. People will gain a deeper understanding of the functions and impact of domestic covert action, and be better able to resist it, if we also address the excuses that government officials offer when their clandestine operations are revealed.

When COINTELPRO was first uncovered, the FBI and the U.S. Justice Department claimed it was needed to prevent violence and to defend the "national security" against totalitarian subversion. Caught running similar operations in the 1980s, they cited the threat of "terrorism." We will see, however, that domestic covert action does not protect against any of this. It actually does the opposite. It subverts democracy and promotes violence and terrorism.

The official excuses for COINTELPRO were flatly rejected by the Senate Intelligence Committee. The Committee found that the program did not combat violence, espionage, or sabotage. Its real purpose was "maintaining the existing social and political order."[174]

The senators dismissed the proffered goal of "protecting national security" as applying at most to operations against the Communist Party. They found that the other targets of domestic covert action have been homegrown radicals not even arguably under the control of an enemy government or organization.[175]

In recent years, as world politics have become more multi-polar, the pretext of national security has largely given way to the new excuse that covert action is needed to combat international terrorism. The political bias of this concept is transparent from its application only to groups such as CISPES, that back foreign movements or governments that the current administration opposes. The concept is never applied to the domestic financiers and publicists for the U.S. client states and CIA-created contras and other phony "freedom fighters" who together account for so much of the world's political violence.[176]

Much of what the U.S. government has cited as international terrorism, such as the "Libyan hit squads" of the early 1980s, turns out to be pure hoax. What remains are largely liberation movements like the African National Congress (ANC) in South Africa and the FMLN in El Salvador. These movements took up arms when military repression (often directed or supported by the United States) made peaceful change impossible. The legitimacy of armed struggle under such conditions has repeatedly been recognized in official United Nations resolutions which are binding on the U.S. government as a matter of international law.[177] Public endorsement and humanitarian aid in support of any political movement, within or outside of our borders, has always been a fundamental democratic right. That a particular administration in Washington slanders such a movement as "terrorist" does not entitle it to obstruct or sabotage constitutionally protected activity on that movement's behalf.

Equally preposterous as a justification for domestic covert action is the official pretense that it helps to prevent violence and terrorism within the United States. Under COINTELPRO, the FBI condoned and supported the racist violence of the Ku Klux Klan, the Secret Army Organization, and other right-wing vigilantes. Throughout the 1980s, it rejected congressional requests that it investigate nationwide political bombings of abortion clinics. Instead, the Bureau "prevents violence" by moving against radical pacifists such as Martin Luther King, Jr. and Maryknoll Sisters.

The record shows that the vast majority of the targets of domestic covert action have engaged only in peaceful protest. They do no harm to anyone's health or safety. The only danger they pose is to the status quo. Their only weapon is the power of their words and the threat of their good example.

Rather than preventing violence, domestic covert action has actually served to promote it. Much of the violence in which U.S. radicals have become involved turns out to have been the responsibility of the FBI or police. A great deal was directly initiated, instigated, incited, or provoked by infiltrators or through other covert operations. Much of the rest has been a response to government repression.

The 1960s radicals who eventually threw rocks, trashed offices, bombed buildings, or shot at policemen started out in peaceful efforts to change public policy and create humane alternatives. It was the government's response that drove them to more drastic action and made it seem the only way left to effect change. The movie "The War at Home"

The federal government has come up with a new way to quarantine political activists:

calling us terrorists.

Meanwhile, the FBI is working to destroy the Left like never before.

They're infiltrating organizations, they're burglarizing offices, they're conducting surveillance.

They're red-baiting, and gay-baiting, and pitting friend against friend.

They have no regard for laws, and less for the Bill of Rights.

So I ask you: why can't the government take care of its own terrorists?

shows how a 1960s pacifist student, Carlton Armstrong, came to bomb an Army research center after he had witnessed and endured repeated brutal beatings during non-violent protests that seemed to have no impact on U.S. policy toward Vietnam. The activists who formed the Weather Underground Organization also had roots in anti-war and civil rights work which came under government attack.

Assata Shakur's autobiography, *Assata,*[178] traces her similar evolution from working in FBI-targeted Black Panther child care centers and health clinics to the Black Liberation Army. Hers is, in this sense, a typical Panther history. While the Black Panther Party always stood for armed self-defense, and a few Panther men were prone to macho posturing and individual acts of violence, the party had no program of armed retaliation during its first four years. That policy was not adopted until late 1970. It came in direct and belated response to years of vicious, armed FBI and police attack on the Panthers and the Black community.

While freely applying its own massive armed force to crush opposition movements at home and abroad, the U.S. government has maneuvered to discredit the legitimate use of force by those who have no other way to resist genocide and fight for freedom. It has colluded with the major media and the academic establishment to cover up official violence and provocation while promoting exaggerated and fabricated accounts which smear movement militancy as "terrorism." This propaganda sets up dissidents for blatant repression and isolates them from the support they need to withstand it.

Domestic covert action thus provides a pretext as well as a vehicle for violent government attacks on progressive movements. Taking into account the political beatings, shootings, and vandalism by the FBI and police, their aid to right-wing vigilantes, their provocation and incitement of brutal assaults on activists, and their outright assassination of movement leaders, these government agencies are far and away the primary source of political violence in the United States. It is they who systematically and aggressively initiate the use of force and intimidation for political ends. Under the guise of combatting terrorism, the FBI and police are—in this fundamental sense—the real terrorists.

The government's secret use of force and fraud to crush political opposition is antithetical to any accepted concept of democracy. In the name of protecting our fundamental freedoms, the FBI and police have in fact subverted them. They have taken the law into their own hands to punish dissident speech and association without the least semblance of due process. By acting covertly, they have insulated themselves from any genuine democratic accountability.

Most people in the United States rightly condemn the secret police (often trained and financed by our government) who terrorize dissident movements in many other countries. Applying the same standards to the FBI and its allies in and out of government, it is hard to escape the conclusion that the situation is not all that different here at home, especially for people of color. The FBI and its associates together perform all the classic functions of a secret police.[179] They may have been somewhat restrained in the post-World War II era of economic abundance and relative ideological consensus, but even then they interrogated, detained, slandered, lied, vandalized, tortured, maimed, and killed. What would they do if millions of people demanded basic change? In the United States today, it is the political police, not the radical activists, who pose the threat to democracy and the danger to law and order.

• Publicly Opposing the Government's Continued Use of Domestic Covert Action

Having exposed domestic covert action as undemocratic and terrorist, it may also be useful, when the energy and resources are available, to engage in public political activity against its continued use. Although public opposition will not be able to eliminate covert repression until we win more systemic change, it can place some limits on what the political police do, and can weaken somewhat their ability to do it. Creative muckraking and organizing can put the FBI and police on the defensive and undermine their morale and legitimacy. It may lead some operations to be abandoned and some operatives to defect. It also serves to deepen popular understanding of the U.S. political system and reinforce activists' awareness of domestic covert action. The following section discusses various approaches to organizing against the government's continued use of such action.

1. Investigative research is crucial if we are to monitor and document the homefront operations of the FBI, CIA, military intelligence, state and local police, "private sector" cops, and right-wing vigilantes. Keep in touch with national groups that do this work (see listing in the back of this book). Get their materials and let them know your experiences and ideas. These groups or a local lawyer can help you use the Freedom of Information Act and other research tools.

2. Public education: Our goal is not merely to prove what the FBI and police do, but to get it across to a broad audience. Experiment with forums, rallies, radio and television, leaflets, pamphlets, comics, cartoons, film, posters, guerrilla theater, and any other avenue that might prove interesting and effective.

3. Support for specific victims of domestic covert action can drive home the danger while reducing somewhat the harm done. Organizing on behalf of break-in targets, grand jury resisters, and defendants in political trials offers a natural forum for public education. It is especially important to publicize the cases of the COINTELPRO targets who remain in prison: Leonard Peltier, Dennis Banks, Geronimo Pratt, Dhoruba Al-Mujahid Bin Wahad, Sundiata Acoli, Herman Bell, Anthony Bottom, Nuh Washington, and so many others. Groups listed in the back can provide information and help you hook up with support committees.

4. Direct action often draws the most attention from the media and can directly impede political police operations. COINTELPRO was initially exposed when confidential files were removed from an FBI office and released to news media. Citizens' arrests, mock trials, picket lines, and civil disobedience have recently greeted CIA recruiters on a number of college campuses. Although the main focus has been on the Agency's international crimes, its domestic activities have also received attention. Similar actions might be organized to protest recruitment by the FBI and police, in conjunction with teach-ins and other educational efforts. Demonstrations against attempts to expand the government's clandestine capability, or against particular FBI, CIA, or police operations, could also raise public consciousness and focus activists' outrage.

5. Lawsuits and legislative campaigns can provide a focus for public education and media coverage. Trials, pretrial discovery, and congressional hearings have proved a valuable source of documents and testimony. Lawsuits can also win financial compensation for some of the people harmed by covert action, and legislative lobbying can help defeat proposals that would protect it (e.g., bills to punish whistle-blowers or cut back public access to information).

Some legislative campaigns and lawsuits have also resulted in laws and court orders which limit political police activity. Although police and intelligence agencies generally find ways around such legal restrictions, they may feel compelled to refrain from some operations which could prove especially embarrassing or to conceal them in ways that backfire. While Acts of Congress never directly stopped U.S. covert action in Nicaragua, for instance, they did lay the basis for the "Contragate" scandal which ultimately helped to undermine the Reagan administration's capacity to intervene.

The value of legal restrictions on covert action will depend on our ability to mobilize continuing, vigilant public pressure for effective enforcement. It is crucial that we resist the temptation to think that the mere existence of laws and court orders means that COINTELPRO-type operations have ended. In deciding whether to take on a lawsuit or

legislative campaign, remember that they are enormously expensive and time-consuming, they can easily be turned into government probes of movement activities, and apparent victories can be undone by judicial reinterpretation. Watch out for bills or proposed judicial decrees which would divide our movements by authorizing covert action against some activists under the guise of protecting others.

A number of these lessons emerge from analysis of the history of the class action lawsuit filed in the mid-1970s to restrict FBI, CIA, and police activity in Chicago. In its early stages, the case yielded a great deal of useful information and publicity. By the time of trial, however, support had dwindled and the suit became a drain on an underpaid and over-burdened legal team. Over the objection of many local activists, a settlement was accepted which protects only those who eschew any law violation or any involvement with a government or organization which the U.S. government labels "terrorist." The effect of the settlement was to legalize government infiltration and disruption of Chicago-area groups that engage in civil disobedience at home or oppose U.S. attacks on progressive governments and national liberation movements abroad.[180]

Some prominent civil libertarians celebrated this agreement and cited it, along with similar legislative and courtroom "victories," as marking the defeat of COINTELPRO-type operations in the United States.

Well into the Reagan years, these influential figures scoffed at warnings that domestic covert action remains a serious threat. Recently obtained FBI documents show, however, that the Bureau's Chicago field office never ceased its clandestine maneuvers. It was deeply involved throughout the 1980s in the Reagan administration's nationally coordinated covert campaign against CISPES and other opponents of U.S. intervention in Central America.[181] The U.S. Court of Appeals has made the settlement of the Chicago class action lawsuit practically ineffective against such campaigns. It ruled that the settlement decree prohibits FBI and police operations only in the unlikely event that they are proved to be based "*solely* on the political views of a group or an individual" and the agencies can conjure up *no* pretext of a "basis in a genuine concern for law enforcement."[182]

6. Coalitions: Direct action, guerrilla theater, postering, and any number of other effective forms of public protest can be done quite well by small affinity groups or ad hoc bands of activists. Major legislative campaigns and lawsuits, however, require a broader and more durable organizational base. Stable centers of public opposition to domestic covert action can serve a number of important functions. Such organizations can raise funds for full-time staff to monitor the political police, organize public events, and publish educational materials. They can cultivate media contacts, providing a steady flow of authoritative background and quotable commentary. They can also counter FBI propaganda and train activists to cope with covert action. Their prominent public presence may in itself serve as some restraint on the FBI and police and offer a form of protection that makes it easier for some operatives to defect.

In most localities, and certainly on a national level, no existing political organization is strong enough to do all this by itself. Our best hope is to form an alliance among individuals and groups who oppose domestic covert action on a variety of grounds. Sustaining such a broad coalition requires that we resist the government's maneuvers to divide us. A stated, long-range goal common to all the COINTELPRO programs was to prevent the development of coalitions within and among dissident movements. The most militant and radical groups, especially supporters of third world liberation, were consistently singled out for direct attack, while it was hinted that things would go easier for those who dissociated from such "violent disruptive elements." The same approach is evident today in government efforts to separate "politically motivated" sanctuary activists from those deemed truly "religious"[183] and to isolate as "terrorists" those who support the national liberation movement in El

Salvador or fight for Black liberation, Puerto Rican independence, or Native American sovereignty here at home.

• Not Letting Political Repression Divert Us From Building Strong Movements for Social Justice

Previous attempts to mobilize public opposition, especially on a local level, indicate that a broad coalition, employing a multi-faceted approach, may be able to impose some limits on government operations to discredit and disrupt our movements. It is clear, however, that we are not now in a position to eliminate such intervention. While fighting hard to end this hidden war at home, we need to take the time to study the forms it takes and prepare ourselves to cope with it effectively.

Above all, it is essential that we resist the temptation to so preoccupy ourselves with repression that we neglect our main goals. Our ability to resist the government's attacks depends ultimately on the strength of our movements. If we deal openly and well with our differences, covert action will not easily disrupt and divide us. If we show respect for the people we live and work with, and help them to fight for their needs, it will be hard for the FBI and police to discredit and isolate us. We will be able, instead, to draw support from our neighbors and co-workers and expose the political police to them. So long as we advocate and organize effectively, no manner of government intervention can stop us.

DOCUMENTS

Memorandum • UNITED STATES GOVERNMENT

CP, USA - COUNTERINTELLIGENCE PROGRAM
INTERNAL SECURITY - C   August 28, 1956

During its investigation of the Communist Party, USA, the Bureau has sought to capitalize on incidents involving the Party and its leaders in order to foster factionalism, bring the Communist Party (CP) and its leaders into disrepute before the American public and cause confusion and dissatisfaction among rank-and-file members of the CP.

Generally, the above action has constituted harrassment rather than disruption, since, for the most part, the Bureau has set up particular incidents, and the attack has been from the outside. At the present time, however, there is existing within the CP a situation resulting from the developments at the 10th Congress of the CP of the Soviet Union and the Government's attack on the Party principally through prosecutions under the Smith act of 1940 and the Internal Security Act of 1950 which is made to order for an all-out disruptive attack against the CP from within. In other words, the Bureau is in a position to initiate, on a broader scale than heretofore attempted, a counterintelligence program against the CP, not by harrassment from the outside, which might only serve to bring the various factions together, but by feeding and fostering from within the internal fight currently raging. ...

ACTION: A memorandum, together with a letter to 12 key offices is being prepared, requesting those offices to submit to the Bureau the identities of certain informants who will be briefed and instructed to embark on a disruptive program within their own clubs, sections, districts or even on a national level. Those informants will raise objections and doubts as to the success of any proposed plan of action by the CP leadership. They will seize every opportunity to carry out the disruptive activity not only at meetings, conventions, et cetera, but also during social and other contacts with CP members and leaders. ...

(Note: These documents have been retyped for legibility and edited for reasons of space.)

Memorandum • UNITED STATES GOVERNMENT

DATE: 11/15/60

GROUPS SEEKING INDEPENDENCE
FOR PUERTO RICO (COUNTERINTELLIGENCE PROGRAM)
SUBVERSIVE CONTROL

...It is believed that upon instituting a counterintelligence program in this field, efforts should be directed with the following aims in mind:

    I. Disruption and discord.

    II. Creating doubts as to the wisdom of remaining in the independence movement.

    III. Causing defections from the independence movement.

The suggested means of obtaining these desired ends are as follows:

1) Exploiting factionalism within an organization. Factionalism is a common fault within pro-independence groups and it is believed that this existing element can be developed, enlarged and exploited... Friction, such as existed between these two at that time, can be exploited through the use of an informant to point out to one, the inefficiency of the others and in general conversation "fan the fire" of existing friction thereby helping to bring about a factional split.

Secondly, the use of handwritten, anonymous letters directed to one group in which the seed of suspicion is planted concerning the real motivation and goal of the other group.

2) Promoting friction between various pro-independence groups...

In this instance the use of informants and anonymous letters could be used, as set forth in number 1 above, and in addition a mimeographed flyer could be utilized in conjunction with the anonymous letters, criticizing the leadership of the organization and giving the impression that it had been prepared by another pro-independence group...

3) Questioning the indiscriminate use of an
organization's money...

In instances such as this, friction between
the members and the leaders can be developed through
the use of informants and anonymous letters.

4) Questioning the wisdom of allowing non-Puer-
to Rican groups to be influential in the independence
movement. ...

In NYC at present, however, [deleted] and his
followers are associating with, and using the
facilities of, the Workers World Party. The WWP is a
splinter group of the Socialist Workers Party and are
known as Marcyites. In an instance such as this, it is
felt that an opportunity is presented whereby
mimeographed flyers could be directed to various individuals of the different pro-independence groups
pointing out the "intrusion" of the WWP and worded in
such a way as to indicate that the SWP was the
originator of the flyer.

The above items are submitted as suggestions
as a beginning. They in no way cover the vast field of
possibilities in the counterintelligence program as
numerous instances will undoubtedly arise from time to
time whereby new ideas can be formulated which can further promote such a program.

SAC, Albany   August 25, 1967

Director, FBI

   COUNTERINTELLIGENCE PROGRAM
   BLACK NATIONALIST - HATE GROUPS
   INTERNAL SECURITY

   ...The purpose of this new counterintelligence
endeavor is to expose, disrupt, misdirect, discredit,
or otherwise neutralize the activities of black
nationalist hate-type organizations and groupings,
their leadership, spokesmen, membership, and supporters, and to counter their propensity for violence
and civil disorder. The activities of all such groups
of intelligence interest to the Bureau must be followed
on a continuous basis so we will be in a position to
promptly take advantage of all opportunities for
counterintelligence and to inspire action in instances
where circumstances warrant. The pernicious background
of such groups, their duplicity, and devious maneuvers
must be exposed to public scrutiny where such publicity
will have a neutralizing effect. Efforts of the various
groups to consolidate their forces or to recruit new or
youthful adherents must be frustrated. No opportunity
should be missed to exploit through counterintelligence
techniques the organizational and personal conflicts of
the leaderships of the groups and where possible an effort should be made to capitalize upon existing conflicts between competing black nationalist
organizations. When an opportunity is apparent to disrupt or neutralize black nationalist, hate-type organizations through the cooperation of established
local news media contacts or through such contact with
sources available to the Seat of Government, in every
instance careful attention must be given to the
proposal to insure the targeted group is disrupted,
ridiculed, or discredited through the publicity and not
merely publicized....

   You are also cautioned that the nature of this
new endeavor is such that under no circumstances should
the existence of the program be made known outside the
Bureau and appropriate within-office security should be
afforded to sensitive operations and techniques con-
sidered under the program.

        No counterintelligence action under this pro-
gram may be initiated by the field without specific
prior Bureau authorization.

COUNTERINTELLIGENCE PROGRAM
BLACK NATIONALIST - HATE GROUPS
RACIAL INTELLIGENCE   3/4/68

BACKGROUND

        ...The Revolutionary Action Movement (RAM), a
pro-Chinese communist group, was active in Philadelphia, Pa., in the summer of 1967. The Philadelphia Office alerted local police, who then put RAM leaders
under close scrutiny. They were arrested on every possible charge until they could no longer make bail. As a
result, RAM leaders spent most of the summer in jail
and no violence traceable to RAM took place. ...

    GOALS

        For maximum effectiveness of the Counterintel-
ligence Program, and to prevent wasted effort, long-
range goals are being set.

        1. Prevent the coalition of militant black
nationalist groups. In unity there is strength; a
truism that is no less valid for all its triteness. An
effective coalition of black nationalist groups might
be the first step toward a real "Mau Mau" in America,
the beginning of a true black revolution.

        2. Prevent the rise of a "messiah" who could
unify, and electrify, the militant black nationalist
movement. Malcolm X might have been such a "messiah;"
he is the martyr of the movement today. Martin Luther
King, Stokely Carmichael and Elijah Muhammed all aspire
to this position. Elijah Muhammed is less of a threat
because of his age. King could be a very real contender
for this position should he abandon his supposed
"obedience" to "white, liberal doctrines" (nonviolence)
and embrace black nationalism. Carmichael has the necessary charisma to be a real threat in this way.

        3. Prevent violence on the part of black
nationalist groups. This is of primary importance, and
is, of course, a goal of our investigative activity; it
should also be a goal of the Counterintelligence Program. Through counterintelligence it should be possible
to pinpoint potential troublemakers and neutralize them
before they exercise their potential for violence.

        4. Prevent militant black nationalist groups
and leaders from gaining respectability, by discrediting them to three separate segments of the community.
The goal of discrediting black nationalists must be

handled tactically in three ways. You must discredit
those groups and individuals to, first, the responsible
Negro community. Second, they must be discredited to
the white community, both the responsible community and
to "liberals" who have vestiges of sympathy for
militant black nationalist[s] simply because they are
Negroes. Third, these groups must be discredited in the
eyes of Negro radicals, the followers of the movement.
This last area requires entirely different tactics from
the first two. Publicity about violent tendencies and
radical statements merely enhances black nationalists
to the last group; it adds "respectability" in a different way.

         5. A final goal should be to prevent the long-
range growth of militant black nationalist organizations, especially among youth. Specific tactics to
prevent these groups from converting young people must
be developed. ...

    TARGETS

         Primary targets of the Counterintelligence Pro-
gram, Black Nationalist-Hate Groups, should be the most
violent and radical groups and their leaders. We should
emphasize those leaders and organizations that are
nationwide in scope and are most capable of disrupting
this country. These targets should include the radical
and violence-prone leaders, members, and followers of
the:

         Student Nonviolent Coordinating Committee (SNCC)
         Southern Christian Leadership Conference (SCLC)
         Revolutionary Action Movement (RAM)
         Nation of Islam (NOI)

         Offices handling these cases and those of
Stokely Carmichael of SNCC, H. Rap Brown of SNCC, Martin Luther King of SCLC, Maxwell Stanford of RAM, and
Elijah Muhammed of NOI, should be alert for counterintelligence suggestions. ...

COUNTERINTELLIGENCE PROGRAM
INTERNAL SECURITY
DISRUPTION OF THE NEW LEFT
(COINTELPRO – NEW LEFT)   7/5/68

Bulet 5/10/68 requested suggestions for counterintelligence action against the New Left. The replies to the Bureau's request have been analyzed and it is felt that the following suggestions for counterintelligence action can be utilized by all offices:

1. Preparation of a leaflet designed to counteract the impression that Students for a Democratic Society (SDS) and other minority groups speak for the majority of students at universities. The leaflet should contain photographs of New Left leadership at the respective university. Naturally, the most obnoxious pictures should be used.

2. The instigating of or the taking advantage of personal conflicts or animosities existing between New Left leaders.

3. The creating of impressions that certain New Left leaders are informants for the Bureau or other law enforcement agencies.

4. The use of articles from student newspapers and/or the "underground press" to show the depravity of New Left leaders and members. In this connection, articles showing advocation of the use of narcotics and free sex are ideal to send to university officials, wealthy donors, members of the legislature and parents of students who are active in New Left matters.

5. Since the use of marijuana and other narcotics is widespread among members of the New Left, you should be alert to opportunities to have them arrested by local authorities on drug charges...

6. The drawing up of anonymous letters regarding individuals active in the New Left. These letters should set out their activities and should be sent to their parents, neighbors and the parents' employers. This could have the effect of forcing the parents to take action.

7. Anonymous letters or leaflets describing faculty members and graduate assistants in the various institutions of higher learning who are active in New Left matters. The activities and associations of the individual should be set out. Anonymous mailings should be made to university officials, members of the state

legislature, Board of Regents, and to the press. Such
letters could be signed "A Concerned Alumni" or "A Concerned Taxpayer."

    8. Whenever New Left groups engage in disrup-
tive activities on college campuses, cooperative press
contacts should be encouraged to emphasize that the disruptive elements constitute a minority of the students
and do not represent the conviction of the majority...

    9. There is a definite hostility among SDS and
other New Left groups toward the Socialist Workers
Party (SWP), the Young Socialist Alliance (YSA), and
the Progressive Labor Party (PLP). This hostility
should be exploited wherever possible.

    10. The field was previously advised that New
Left groups are attempting to open coffeehouses near
military bases in order to influence members of the
Armed Forces. Wherever these coffeehouses are, friendly
news media should be alerted to them and their purpose.
In addition, various drugs, such as marijuana, will
probably be utilized by individuals running the coffeehouses or frequenting them. Local law enforcement
authorities should be promptly advised whenever you
receive an indication that this is being done.

    11. Consider the use of cartoons, photographs,
and anonymous letters which will have the effect of
ridiculing the New Left. Ridicule is one of the most
potent weapons which we can use against it.

    12. Be alert for opportunities to confuse and
disrupt New Left activities by misinformation. For example, when events are planned, notification that the
event has been cancelled or postponed could be sent to
various individuals. ...

NOTES

FBI documents referred to without other citation are in the author's files and the FBI Reading Room in Washington, D.C. Many of these, as well as documents cited to other sources, will be in Churchill and Vander Wall, eds., *COINTELPRO Papers: Documents from the FBI's Secret War on Domestic Dissent* (South End Press, 1989). The notes use the following shorthand:

AFSC: *The Police Threat to Political Liberty* (American Friends Service Committee, 1979).

Documents: Macy, Christy, and Susan Kaplan, eds., *Documents: A Shocking Collection of Memoranda, Letters, and Telexes from the Secret Files of the American Intelligence Community* (Penguin Books, 1980).

Iron Fist: *The Iron Fist and the Velvet Glove: An Analysis of the U.S. Police* (Center for Research on Criminal Justice, 1975)

NLG: *Counterintelligence: A Documentary Look at America's Secret Police* (National Lawyers Guild, 1982).

Senate II, Senate III, Senate VI: *Books II, III, and VI of Intelligence Activities and the Rights of Americans, Final Report of the Select Committee to Study Government Operations with Respect to Intelligence Activities, U.S. Senate* (94th Cong., 2d Sess. Rep. No. 94-755, U.S. Government Printing Office, 1976).

***

1. Buitrago, Ann Mari, *Report on CISPES Files Maintained by FBI Headquarters and Released Under the Freedom of Information Act* (Fund for Open Information and Accountability, Inc., 1988); *GROUPS INCLUDED IN THE CISPES FILES OBTAINED FROM FBI HEADQUARTERS,* (Center for Constitutional Rights, 1988); *SELECTED HEADQUARTERS CISPES DOCUMENTS* (Center for Constitutional Rights, 1988); Ridgeway, James, "Abroad at Home: The FBI's Dirty War," *Village Voice*, Feb. 9, 1988, and "FBI Spies on Three in Congress," *Village Voice*, March 31, 1987.

2. Harlan, Christi, "The Informant Left Out in the Cold," *Dallas Morning News*, April 6, 1986, p.l; King, Wayne, "An FBI Inquiry Fed by Informer Emerges in Analysis of Documents," *New York Times*, Feb. 13, 1988, p. 33; Gelbspan, Ross, "Documents show Moon group aided FBI," *Boston Globe*, April 1988, p.l; Ridgeway, James, "Spooking the Left," *Village Voice*, March 3, 1987; *Testimony of the Center for Constitutional Rights before the House Committee on the Judiciary, Subcommittee on Civil and Constitutional Rights*, Feb. 20, 1987, pp. 19-21; Bielski, Vince, Cindy Forster, and Dennis Bernstein, "The Death Squads Hit Home," *The Progressive*, Oct. 16, 1987.

3. Tolan, Sandy, and Carol Ann Bassett, "Operation Sojourner: Informers in the Sanctuary Movement," *Nation*, July 20/27, 1985; Ovryn, Rachel, "Operation Sojourner: Targeting the Sanctuary Movement," *Covert Action Information Bulletin* No. 24 (Summer 1985); Crittenden, Ann, *Sanctuary* (Weidenfeld & Nicolson, 1988).

4. Anderson, Jack, "Navy Infiltrates Group Opposing Nuclear Arms," *Washington Post*, Jan. 28, 1984; Peck, Keenen, "The Take-Charge Gang," *The Progressive*, May 1985.

5. "FBI Spies on Peace Groups," *Movement Support Network News*, April 1986.

6. Ungar, Sanford J., "The FBI on the Defensive Again," *The New York Times Magazine*, May 15, 1988.

7. Jones, Jeff, "City Settles with Albany Activists," *Guardian*, Aug. 17, 1988; interview with CDCAAR attorney Lanny Walter, Sept. 1988.

8. Donner, Frank, "Travelers' Warning for Nicaragua," *The Nation*, July 6/13, 1985; Ridgeway, James, "Home is Where the Covert Action Is," *Village Voice*, Dec. 16, 1986; *Harassment Update*, 13th Ed., April 1988 (Movement Support Network).

9. Cole, David, "The Deportation of a Poet," *The Nation*, June 25, 1988.

10. Ridgeway, James, "Home is Where the Covert Action Is," *Village Voice*, Dec. 16, 1986; *Update on Political Break-Ins*, May 1988 (Movement Support Network); *Harassment Update*, 13th Ed.; Kohn, Alfie, "Political Burglaries: The Return of COINTELPRO?" *Nation*, January 25, 1986; Schneider, Keith, "Pattern is Seen in Break-Ins at Latin Policy Groups," *New York Times*, December 3, 1986, p. A13; Gelbspan, Ross, "A Political Thread Entwines Break-ins," *Boston Globe*, January 18, 1987; Gelbspan, Ross, "Central America Activists Call for Probe of Break-ins," *Boston Globe*, December 7, 1986, p. 28.

11. Soble, Ronald, "Deportation of Alleged PLO Members Tied to FBI Report," *Los Angeles Times*, Feb. 22, 1987, p. 3; Gottleib, Jeff, "Immigrants say they're target of FBI harassment," *Los Angeles Herald Examiner*, May 22, 1988, p.A3; Butterfield, Jeanne, "Arrested Palestinians Under Surveillance for Three Years," *Guardian*, April 8, 1987, p. 7; Madi, Salim, "Secret Plan Targets Arabs," *Guardian*, Feb. 18, 1987, p. 1; interview with Linda Lotz, Field Representative, American Friends Service Committee, June 1988.

12. López, Alfredo, *Doña Licha's Island: Modern Colonialism in Puerto Rico* (South End Press, 1987), pp. 140-142; "FBI Raids Homes of Independentistas," *Movement Support Network News*, Autumn 1985; interview with defense attorney Linda Backiel, Oct. 1988.

13. Tate, Greg, "Dirty Tricks vs. the Right to Dissent," *Village Voice*, July 2, 1985; Interview with NY8+ defendant and attorney, Roger Wareham, July 1988.

14. Collins, Sheila, *The Rainbow Challenge* (Monthly Review Press, 1986), p. 293. See also: Tullos, Allen, "Voting Rights Activists Acquitted," *The Nation*, August 3/10, 1985.

15. Cowan, Paul, Nick Egleson, and Nat Hentoff, *State Secrets: Police Surveillance in America* (Holt, Rinehart & Winston, 1974).

16. E.g., Wall, Robert, "Why I Got Out of It," *New York Review of Books*, Jan. 27, 1972, reprinted in Watters, Pat, and Stephen Gillers, *Investigating the FBI* (Ballantine Books, 1973), pp. 336-350, and in Platt, Anthony, and Lynn Cooper, *Policing America* (Prentice Hall, 1974), pp. 105-118.

17. This and the following history is based on Zinn, Howard, *A People's History of the United States* (Harper and Row, 1980), pp. 529ff. For the text of the Papers: *The Pentagon Papers* (Bantam Books, 1971).

18. Zinn, p. 542.

19. Zinn, p. 543; Johnson, Loch, *A Season of Inquiry: The Senate Intelligence Investigation* (University of Kentucky Press, 1985), pp. 221, 271; Hersh, Seymour, *The Price of Power* (Simon and Schuster, 1983) p. 295.

20. Zinn, p. 543. The Report appeared in *Village Voice*, Feb. 16 and 23, 1976.

21. Donner, Frank, *The Age of Surveillance* (Vintage, 1981) pp. 170, 175; *AFSC*, pp. 46,54-55,78.

22. Statement of Retired FBI Special Agent Arthur Murtagh, *U.S. Intelligence Agencies and Activities: Domestic Intelligence Programs; Hearings before the Select Committee on Intelligence, U.S. House of Representatives*, Part 3, (94th Cong. lst Sess., U.S. Government Printing Office, 1976), p. 1044; Interview with Retired FBI Special Agent Wes Swearingen, June 1979.

23. Biskind, Peter, "Inside the FBI," *Seven Days*, May 7, 1978, reprinted in *NLG*, p. 103.

24. FBI letter, 8/25/67, excerpted on p. 77 of this book; reprinted in *NLG*, p. 12.

84   **Brian Glick**

25. *Ibid.*

26. *Senate III*, p. 4.

27. *Senate III*, p. 8.

28. This list of targets and the following overview of COINTELPRO programs is based on: the sources listed in the back of this book; Horrock, Nicholas, "FBI Releases Most Files on Its Programs to Disrupt Dissident Groups," *New York Times*, Nov. 22, 1977, p. 26; and the author's research at the FBI Reading Room in Washington, D.C.

29. The quote is from FBI Airtel, 3/4/68, excerpted on p. 78-79 of this book; reprinted in *NLG*, p. 17. See generally: *Senate III*, pp. 79-184; Garrow, David, *The FBI and Martin Luther King, Jr.* (W.W. Norton & Co., 1981) and *Bearing the Cross: Martin Luther King and the Southern Christian Leadership Conference* (Vintage, 1988).

30. This section is based on the sources listed in the back of this book, augmented by the author's own experiences and discussions with other 1960s activists.

31. Cluster, Dick, "It Did Make A Difference," in Cluster, ed., *They Should Have Served That Cup of Coffee* (South End Press, 1979), p. 136.

32. See FBI Memorandum and Airtel in *NLG*, pp. 9-10.

33. *Documents*, pp. 178-180; *Senate III*, pp. 135-161; Donner, pp. 214-217; Garrow, pp. 125-134.

34. E.g., Gregory, Dick, and Mark Lane, *Code Name "Zorro"* (Prentice Hall, 1977); T'Shaka, Oba, *The Political Legacy of Malcolm X* (Third World Press, 1983), pp. 217-240; Breitman, George, Herman Porter, and Baxter Smith, *The Assassination of Malcolm X* (Pathfinder Press, 1976).

35. Rips, Geoffrey, "The Campaign Against the Underground Press" (a Pen American Center Report), in *UnAmerican Activities* (City Lights Books, 1981); Mackenzie, Angus, "Sabotaging the Dissident Press," *Columbia Journalism Review*, March 3, 1981; Armstrong, David, *A Trumpet to Arms: Alternative Media in America* (South End Press, 1981), pp. 137ff.

36. *Senate III*, pp. 185-223 ("The FBI's Covert Action Program to Destroy the Black Panther Party"); Churchill, Ward, and James Vander Wall, *Agents of Repression: The FBI's Secret War Against The Black Panther Party and the American Indian Movement* (South End Press, 1988), pp. 63-99.

37. Zinn, pp. 529-544.

38. *Senate III*, pp. 76-77; Donner, pp. 73-74, 131.

39. Dinges, John, and Jeff Stein, "Webster's Mission: Burying Hoover's Ghost," *Boston Globe Magazine*, May 1, 1983.

40. *Iron Fist*, pp. 31-86; *AFSC*, pp. 14-16,24-61; Burkholder, Steve, "Red Squads on the Prowl: Still Spying After All These Years," *The Progressive*, Oct. 1988.

41. On CIA domestic covert operations, see: *Senate III*, pp. 679-732; Wise, David, *The American Police State* (Random House, 1976), pp. 183-257; McGehee, Ralph, *Deadly Deceits: My 25 Years With the CIA* (Sheridan Square Publ. 1983), pp.ix-xii, 81-86.

42. Peck, pp. 19-20; Butz, Tim, "Garden Plot & SWAT: U.S. Police as New Action Army," *Counterspy*, Winter 1976; Lawrence, Ken, "The New State Repression," *Covert Action Information Bulletin*, Summer 1985. The manuals are cited at note 98.

43. Memorandum, 4/27/71, and Airtel, 4/28/71, in Perkus, Cathy, *COINTELPRO: The FBI's Secret War on Political Freedom* (Monad Press, 1975), pp. 26-27.

44. Churchill and Vander Wall, pp. 135-349; Johansen, Bruce, and Roberto Maestas, *Wasi'Chu: The Continuing Indian Wars* (Monthly Review Press, 1979); Matthiessen, Peter, *In the Spirit of Crazy Horse* (Viking Press, 1984); Messerschmidt, Jim, *The Trial of Leonard Peltier* (South End Press, 1983); Weyler, Rex, *Blood of the Land: The Government and Corporate War Against the American Indian Movement* (Vintage Books, 1984); Amnesty International, *Proposal for a Commission of Inquiry into the Effect of Domestic Intelligence Activities on Criminal Trials in the United States of America* (1981) pp. 41-46.

45. Churchill and Vander Wall, p. 175; Johansen and Maestas, p. 84.

46. Johansen amd Maestas, pp. 95-96.

47. *AFSC*, pp. 59,67; Rapoport, Roger, "Meet America's Meanest Dirty Trickster," *Mother Jones*, April 1977.

48. Hinds, Lennox, *Illusions of Justice: Human Rights Violations in the United States* (Univ. of Iowa School of Social Work, 1978), pp. 165-204.

49. Hinds, pp. 258-263, augmented by the author's experience as counsel for the RNA in its Freedom of Information Act litigation. See also: Edwards, Allison, "FBI Disrupts Republic of New Africa," *National Lawyers Guild Notes*, Oct. 1978.

50. Durden-Smith, Jo, *Who Killed George Jackson?* (Alfred A. Knopf, 1976); Mann, Eric, *Comrade George: An Investigation into the Life, Political Thought, and Assassination of George Jackson* (Harper and Row, 1974).

51. The account of Geronimo Pratt's case is based on the author's experience as a member the legal team handling Pratt's efforts to reopen his case. See also: Churchill and Vander Wall, pp. 77-94; Amnesty International, pp. 21-33; CBS television, *60 Minutes*, Nov. 29, 1987.

52. Moore, Dhoruba, "Strategies of Repression Against the Black Movement," *Black Scholar*, May-June 1981; Shakur, Assata, *Assata: An Autobiography* (Lawrence Hill & Co., 1987); Bukhari, Safiya, *Lest We Forget* (Black Community News Service, 1985).

53. This paragraph is based on the author's experience as counsel for the NY3 in their efforts to obtain a new trial. Pleadings and documents are on file at the Cardozo Law School Criminal Law Clinic in New York City. An excellent video is available from Paper Tiger TV, 339 Lafayette St. NY, NY 10012.

54. "Progressive Chicanos Sue FBI, CIA," *Black Panther Newspaper*, Aug. 20, 1977, p. 1.

55. Donner, pp. 347-348; *Iron Fist*, p. 135.

56. *U.S. v. Martínez, Federal Reporter, 2d Series*, vol. 667, p. 886; Martínez, Elizabeth, "The Kiko Martínez Case," *Crime and Social Justice*, Summer 1982 and Summer 1983.

57. Anglada López, Rafael, "A New Wave of Repression?" *Claridad*, Oct. 28/Nov. 3, 1983, p. 9; Donner, pp. 384-385; documents on file at the People's Law Office, Chicago.

58. Nelson, Anne, *Murder Under Two Flags: The US, Puerto Rico, and the Cerro Marravilla Cover-Up* (Ticknor & Fields, 1986); Suárez, Manuel, "Ex-Puerto Rican Police Agent Guilty in Slaying of 2 Radicals," *New York Times*, March 19,1988; López, Alfredo, *Doña Licha's Island: Modern Colonialism in Puerto Rico* (South End Press, 1987), p. 149; Berkan, Judy, "The Crime of Cerro Maravilla," *Puerto Rico Libre*, May-June 1979.

59. National Committee to Free Puerto Rican Prisoners of War, *Petition to the United Nations*, May 16, 1980, p. 35.

60. Rips, p. 129.

61. Gregory-Lewis, Sasha, "Revelations of a Gay Informant," *The Advocate*, March 9, 1977; "Report of the House Select Committee on Intelligence," *Village Voice*, Feb. 16, 1976, p. 91.

62. Harris, Richard, *Freedom Spent* (Little, Brown, 1975), pp. 273-378; Donner, p. 384.

63. Viorst, Milton, "FBI Mayhem," *New York Review of Books*, March 18, 1976; Donner, pp. 440-446.

64. Donner, pp. 373-376; Donner, Frank, "The Confessions of an FBI Informer," *Harper's Magazine*, Dec. 1972.

65. Crewdson, John, "FBI Reportedly Harassed Radicals After Spy Program Ended," *New York Times*, March 23, 1975, p. 33.

66. *UE News*, March 1975; Lawrence, Ken, *Profile of an FBI Provocateur* (Anti-Repression Resource Team, 1981).

67. Stein, Jeffrey, "Karen Silkwood: The Deepening Mystery," *The Progressive*, Jan. 1981; Rashke, Richard, *The Killing of Karen Silkwood* (Houghton Mifflin, 1981); Kohn, Howard, *Who Killed Karen Silkwood?* (Summit Books, 1981).

68. Taylor, G. Flint, "Waller v. Butkovich," *Police Misconduct and Civil Rights Law Reporter*, Jan./Feb. 1986; Greensboro Justice Fund, *Greensboro Civil Rights Suit: Confronting America's Death Squads* and *The Greensboro Civil Rights Suit: The Struggle Against Racist Violence.*

69. Holowach, Frank, "The NASSCO Case: A Case Study in Infiltration and Entrapment," *Covert Action Information Bulletin*, Summer 1985; Lindsey, Robert, "Bombing Plot Trial Nears End on Coast," *New York Times*, June 3, 1981, p.A17; "Ironworkers Move to Expel Five Activists at NASSCO Shipyard," *Labor Notes*, July 21, 1982; interview with attorney Leonard Weinglass, May 1988.

70. Intelligence Identities Protection Act of 1982, Title 50, *United States Code*, sec. 421(c). See generally: Pell, Eve, *The Big Chill* (Beacon Press, 1984), pp. 29-95; *Government Decisions Without Democracy* (People for the American Way, 1987).

71. *Senate III*, p. 3.

72. National Security Act of 1947, Title 50, *United States Code*, sec. 403(d)(3).

73. Pell, pp. 193-194.

74. Pasztor, Andy, "Walsh Probes Whether North, Secord Spied on Reagan Critics, Sources Say," *Wall Street Journal*, Dec. 7, 1987, p. 54; Picharallo, Joe, "Contra Funds Used to Fight Suit," *Washington Post*, June 29, 1987, p.A3; "North Spies on Institute," *Convergence* (Christic Institute), Spring 1988.

75. Chardy, Alphonso, "Reagan advisers ran 'secret' government," *Miami Herald*, July 5, 1987, p.lA; Ridgeway, James, "Return of the Night Animals," *Village Voice*, Feb. 26, 1985; Peck, Keenen, "The Take-Charge Gang," *The Progressive*, May 1985.

76. *Senate II*, p. 66.

77. See *Senate VI* and sources listed in the back of this book.

78. Wolfe, Alan, *The Seamy Side of Democracy* (Longman, 1978), pp. 86-88.

79. Zinn, pp. 363-364; Cook, Fred J., *The FBI Nobody Knows* (Macmillan, 1964), pp. 61-70; Ungar, Sanford J., *FBI* (Little, Brown & Co., 1975), pp. 41-42.

80. Powers, Richard Gid, *Secrecy and Power: The Life of J.Edgar Hoover* (Free Press, 1987), pp. 56-129; Goldstein, Robert Justin, *Political Repression in Modern America* (Schenkman Publishing, 1978), pp. 144-163.

81. Railway: Ungar, p. 46; Sacco & Vanzetti: Goldstein, p. 169.

82. Hill, Robert A., " 'The Foremost Radical Among His Race:' Marcus Garvey and the Black Scare, 1918-1921," *Prologue*, Winter 1984.

83. Powers, 179-227; Cook, pp. 146-204; Sherrill, Robert, "The Selling of The FBI," in Gillers and Waters, pp. 23-44.

84. *Senate III*, pp. 392-396.

85. *Senate II*, p. 22.

86. Cook, pp. 270-302; Theoharis, Athan, and John Stuart Cox, *The Boss: J. Edgar Hoover and the Great American Inquisition*, (Temple Univ. Press, 1988), pp. 250-254, 280-294; O'Reilly, Kenneth, *Hoover and the UnAmericans* (Temple Univ. Press, 1983).

87. Theoharis, Athan, ed., *Beyond the Hiss Case: The FBI, Congress & the Cold War* (Temple Univ. Press, 1982), chs.6-8; Cook, pp. 303-327, 362-376; Schneir, Walter and Miriam, *Invitation to an Inquest* (Pantheon, 1983).

88. *Senate II*, pp. 30-33,46-49; *Senate III*, pp. 416422,448-457.

89. Waltzer, Kenneth, "The FBI, Congressman Vito Marcantonio, and the American Labor Party," in Theoharis, ed.; Theoharis and Cox, p. 144n.

WAR AT HOME 87

90. Mitgang, Herbert, *Dangerous Dossiers: Exposing the Secret War Against America's Greatest Authors* (Donald I. Fine, 1988) pp. 31-33; Theoharis and Cox, p. 255.

91. Donner, 144-145; Bailey, Percival, "The Case of the National Lawyers Guild," in Theoharis, ed.; D'Emilio, John, *Sexual Politics, Sexual Communities* (Univ. of Chicago Press, 1983), p. 124; Bennett, Sara, "New Info Disclosed on Surveillance of Lesbians and Gays," *Quash: Newletter of the National Lawyers Guild Grand Jury Project*, Aug./Sept. 1982.

92. *Senate II*, pp. 38,61-62; Crewdson, John, "Details on FBI's Illegal Break-Ins Given to Justice Dept.," *New York Times*, Jan. 27, 1979; Sector, Bob, "FBI 'Bag Squads' Called Common: Former Agent Tells of Break-Ins by Thousands," *Los Angeles Times*, Feb. 2, 1979, p. l; Marro, Anthony, "FBI Break-in Policy," in Theoharis, ed., pp. 96-99.

93. *Senate III*, pp. 417-422; Hedgepeth, William, "America's Concentration Camps: The Rumors and the Realities," *Look Magazine*, May 28, 1968; Ross, Caroline, and Ken Lawrence, *J. Edgar Hoover's Detention Plan* (American Friends Service Committee, 1978).

94. *Senate II*, p. 66.

95. *Ibid.*

96. FBI Memorandum, 8/28/56, excerpted on p. 74 of this book; reprinted in *Hearings before the U.S. Senate Select Committee to Study Government Operations with Respect to Intelligence Activities, Vol. 6* (94th Cong. 1st Sess., U.S. Gov. Printing Office, 1975), p. 372.

97. Airtel reproduced in *NLG*, p. 104.

98. Kitson (Stackpole Books, 1971), p. 71. See also: Evelegh, Robin, *Peace-Keeping in a Democratic Society* (C. Hurst & Co., 1978); Lawrence, Ken, "The New State Repression, *Covert Action Information Bulletin*, Summer 1985; Klare, Michael, and Peter Kornbluth, eds, *Low Intensity Warfare* (Pantheon, 1988); Miles, Sara, "The Real War: Low Intensity Conflict in Central America," *NACLA Report on the Americas*, April/May 1986.

99. Ungar, Sanford J., "The FBI on the Defensive Again, *New York Times Magazine*, May 15, 1988, p. 75; Shenon, Philip, "FBI Agent Admits Harassing Blacks," *New York Times*, July 5, 1988, p. 1; Shenon, Philip, "Judge Finds FBI Is Discriminatory," *New York Times*, Oct. 1, 1988, p. 1.

100. FBI Memorandum cited at note 96.

101. Donner, pp. 133-138; *Iron Fist*, pp. 133-135; Goldstein, pp. 473-477; *Senate III*, pp. 225-247; Cowan, et al., pp. 221-257; Chevigny, Paul, *Cops and Rebels: A Study of Provocation* (Pantheon, 1972).

102. Donner, p. 136.

103. FBI Memorandum in Rips, pp. 68-69.

104. Letter from FBI Director to New York Field Office, Aug. 24, 1970.

105. FBI Memorandum in *NLG*, pp. 59-60.

106. *Senate III*, p. 46.

107. Letter from FBI Director to Washington Field Office, July 1, 1968; Memorandum from Washington Field Office to FBI Director, July 9, 1968; Memorandum from New York Field Office to FBI Director, July 10, 1968. Portions of these documents are in *NLG*, p. 58.

108. Donner, 191-194.

109. *Senate III*, pp. 35-36, 218-220; *Documents*, pp. 110-112; Berlet, Chip, "COINTELPRO: What the (Deleted) Was It?--Media Op," *The Public Eye*, April 1978.

110. Richards, David, *Played Out: The Jean Seberg Story* (Random House, 1981), pp. 234-269; Donner, p. 237.

111. *Senate III*, pp. 37-40, 189-195; Donner, pp. 221-223; *NLG*, pp. 38-39.

112. *Senate III*, p. 210; Donner, p. 225.

113. E.g., Wall, "Special Agent for the FBI," in Platt and Cooper, p. 109.

114. The quote and the pre-reunion version appear in Gitlin, Todd, *The Sixties* (Bantam Books, 1987), pp. 363-364. The account of the reunion, where Gitlin also first heard the true story, is based on my experience as a participant.

115. *Documents*, pp. 142-145; Lewis, Anthony, "Mocking the Law," *New York Times*, June 11, 1984.

116. Wall, in Watters and Gillers, p. 341, and in Platt and Cooper, p. 109; Rips, p. 105.

117. *Senate III*, pp. 200-207.

118. *Senate III*, p. 43.

119. Airtels between New York Field Office and FBI Director, Oct. 17, 21, 25, 1968.

120. *Senate III*, pp. 52-55; *Documents*, pp. 141-142, 145-147.

121. *Senate III*, p. 199, n. 60; Carson, Clayborne, *In Struggle: SNCC and the Black Awakening of the 1960s* (Harvard Univ. Press, 1981), p. 284.

122. Carson, p. 284.

123. FBI Memorandum in *NLG*, p. 41.

124. *Senate III*, pp. 195-198; Churchill and Vander Wall, pp. 65-66.

125. *Senate III*, pp. 8, 29-30, 34, 56-57, 60-61, 140-145, 172-178, 208-213; *Documents*, pp. 148-149.

126. *Senate III*, pp. 56, 177-178; Donner, p. 233; Moore, p. 11.

127. Rips, pp. 96-99, Mackenzie, pp. 10-11; Armstrong, pp. 146,150.

128. *Senate III*, pp. 559-677; Wise, pp. 399-400.

129. *Senate III*, pp. 45-46.

130. "COINTELPRO En Puerto Rico: Documentos Secretos FBI," *Pensamiento Crítico*, Summer 1979; Neufeld, Russell, "COINTELPRO in Puerto Rico," *Quash: Newsletter of the National Lawyers Guild Grand Jury Project*, Aug./Sept. 1982; *Documents*, pp. 176-178.

131. Interview with Mike Spiegel, SDS National Secretary, 1967-68, SDS Washington, D.C. Regional Organizer, 1968-69.

132. *Senate III*, pp. 31-32.

133. Lawrence, Ken, "Mail Surveillance," *Covert Action Information Bulletin*, April 1981; Lotz, Linda, *Bugs, Taps and Infiltrators: What to Do About Political Spying* (National Lawyers Guild Civil Liberties Commitee, 1988).

134. *AFSC*, pp. 65-67.

135. FBI memorandum in Cowan, Egelson, and Hentoff, p. 139.

136. Donner, pp. 353-385; Goldstein, pp. 493-494.

137. *Senate III*, pp. 833-920; Donner, pp. 321-352; Wise, pp. 322-351.

138. *Senate III*, p. 57; *Documents*, pp. 140-141.

139. See FBI Memorandum cited at note 29 above.

140. FBI Airtel in *NLG*, p. 56.

141. Rips, pp. 82-124.

142. *Senate III*, p. 217.

143. Wolfe, pp. 41-43.

144. Mitford, Jessica, *The Trial of Dr. Spock* (Knopf, 1969); Nelson, Jack, and Ronald Ostrow, *The FBI and the Berrigans* (Coward, McCann & Geoghegan, 1972); Epstein, Jason, *The Great Conspiracy Trial* (Vintage, 1971); Carson, pp. 252-257, 289-298; Brown, H. Rap, *Die Nigger Die!* (Dial Press, 1969); Davis, Angela, et al., *If They Come in the Morning* (Signet, 1971).

145. Goldstein, pp. 529-530; Churchill and Vander Wall, pp. 63-99; Freed, Donald, *Agony in New Haven: The Trial of Bobby Seale, Erica Huggins, and the Black Panther Party*

(Simon & Schuster, 1973); Zimroth, Peter, *Perversions of Justice: The Prosecution and Acquittal of the Panther 21* (Viking Press, 1974); Kempton, Murray, *The Briar Patch* (Dutton, 1973); Seale, Bobby, *Seize the Time* (Vintage Books, 1970), pp. 289-361.

146. FBI Memorandum, San Diego Field Office to Director, 2/3/69, quoted in Amnesty International, p. 20.

147. Wolfe, p. 41.

148. Copeland, Vincent, *The Crime of Martin Sostre* (McGraw Hill, 1970); Goldstein, p. 514.

149. Keeting, Edward, *Free Huey! The True Story of the Trial of Huey Newton* (Ramparts Press, 1971); Churchill and Vander Wall, p. 61.

150. Goldstein, p. 514.

151. Rips, pp. 103-104.

152. Amnesty International, pp. 12-14.

153. Jackson, George, *Soledad Brother: The Prison Letters of George Jackson* (Bantam Books, 1970); Armstrong, Gregory, *The Dragon Has Come: The Last Fourteen Months in the Life of George Jackson* (Harper and Row, 1974).

154. Bergman, Lowell, and David Weir, "Revolution on Ice: How the Black Panthers Lost the FBI's War of Dirty Tricks," *Rolling Stone*, Sept. 9, 1976.

155. Airtel from San Francisco Field Office to FBI Director, 4/3/68, p. 7.

156. Gregory: *NLG*, p. 22; Hoodwink: *Senate III*, p. 50; Donner, pp. 189-190.

157. *Senate III*, pp. 192-193.

158. FBI memoranda: New York Field Office to Director, 9/10/69; Director to New York, 9/23/69; New York to Director, 5/21/70.

159. *Senate III*, pp. 267-270; Viorst, *New York Review of Books*; Donner, pp. 440-446; Rips, 130-134.

160. Donner, pp. 427-430; Rips, pp. 117-120.

161. Goldstein, p. 445. See generally: *NLG*, pp. xiii, 4-5; *Senate III, pp. 239-244*; Donner, pp. 207-208.

162. *Senate III*, pp. 353-371; Donner, pp. 130-132; and sources listed in note 92. The operation against the Progressive Labor Party was described in an interview with Ken Lawrence.

163. See sources at note 92.

164. See sources at note 35.

165. Goldstein, pp. 526-527.

166. Rips, p. 112.

167. Goldstein, pp. 509-513; *Petition to the United Nations*, p. 24.

168. Sale, Kirkpatrick, *SDS* (Random House, 1973), p. 641n.

169. Bergman and Weir, *Rolling Stone*.

170. The account that follows is based on Churchill and Vander Wall, pp. 64-77, and Donner, pp. 226-230.

171. Wilkins, Roy, and Ramsey Clark, Chairmen, *Search and Destroy: A Report by the Commission on Inquiry into the Black Panthers and the Police* (Harper and Row, 1973). The opinion of the U.S. Court of Appeals for the Seventh Circuit, *Hampton v. Hanrahan*, is in the *Federal Reporter, 2d Series*, vol.600 (1979), starting at p. 600.

172. See sources listed at note 34.

173. Churchill and Vander Wall, pp. 82-84.

174. *Senate III*, pp. 6-7.

175. *Senate III*, pp. 5-6.

176. See Falk, Richard, *Revolutionaries and Functionaries: The Dual Face of Terrorism* (E.P.Dutton, 1988); Chomsky, Noam, *Pirates and Emperors: International Terrorism in the Real World* (Claremont Research and Publications, 1986), Herman, Edward, "Terrorism & Retaliation," *Zeta*, April 1988, and "Lemoynespeak," *Zeta*, May 1988, and *The Real Terror Network: Terrorism in Fact and Propaganda* (South End Press, 1982); Chomsky and Herman, *The Washington Connection and Third World Fascism* (South End Press, 1979).

177. See especially General Assembly Resolution 33/24 (Dec. 8, 1978); also, Res. 32/14 (Nov. 7, 1977), Res. 31/34 (Nov. 30, 1976), Res. 33/82 (Nov. 1975); Res. 27/08 (Dec. 14, 1970).

178. *Assata: An Autobiography* (Lawrence Hill & Co., 1987).

179. Cf. Wise, pp. 311, 398; *AFSC*, p. 4.

180. "The Red Squads Settlement Controversy," *The Nation*, July 11-18, 1981.

181. See sources at note 1.

182. *Alliance to End Repression v. City of Chicago, Federal Reporter, 2d Series*, vol. 742 (1984), p. 1015 (emphasis added).

183. See Golden, Renny, "Sanctuary: Choosing Sides," *Socialist Review*, No. 90.

FURTHER READING

American Friends Service Committee, *The Police Threat to Political Liberty*, Philadelphia: 1979.

Amnesty International, *A proposal for a commission of inquiry into the effect of domestic intelligence activities on criminal trials in the United States of America*, London: 1981.

Carson, Claybourne, *In Struggle: SNCC and the Black Awakening of the 1960s*, Cambridge, MA: Harvard University Press, 1981.

Center for Research on Criminal Justice, *The Iron Fist and the Velvet Glove: An Analysis of the U.S. Police*, Berkeley, CA: 1975.

Chomsky, Noam, "Introduction" to *COINTELPRO: The FBI's Secret War on Political Freedom*, Blackstock, ed., New York: Vintage Books, 1976.

Churchill, Ward, and Vander Wall, Jim, *Agents of Repression: FBI Attacks on the Black Panthers and the American Indian Movement*, Boston: South End Press, 1988.

Churchill, Ward, and Vander Wall, Jim, *COINTELPRO Papers*, Boston: South End Press, 1989.

Donner, Frank, *The Age of Surveillance: The Aims and Methods of America's Political Intelligence System* , New York: Vintage Books, 1981.

Goldstein, Robert, *Political Repression in Modern America: 1870 to the Present*, Cambridge, MA: Schenkman Publishing Co., 1978.

López, Alfredo, *Doña Licha's Island: Modern Colonialism in Puerto Rico*, Boston: South End Press, 1987.

Moore, Richard "Dhoruba," "Strategies of Repression Against the Black Movement," *The Black Scholar*, May-June 1981.

U.S. Senate Select Committee to Study Government Operations with Respect to Intelligence Activities, *Intelligence Activities and the Rights of Americans*, Books II, III, & VI (94th Cong. 2d Session, Report No. 94-755), Washington, DC: U.S. Government Printing Office, 1976.

Wise, David, *The American Police State: The Government Against the People*, New York: Random House, 1975.

Wolfe, Alan, *The Seamy Side of Democracy: Repression in America*, New York: Longman, Inc., 1978.

Zinn, Howard, *A People's History of the United States*, New York: Harper & Row, 1980.

ABOUT THE AUTHOR

Brian Glick is a lawyer who was active in SDS and the civil rights and antiwar movemements of the 1960s, and who continues to work in the social justice and anti-intervention movements. Co-author of *The Bust Book: What to Do Until the Lawyer Comes* and *The Jailhouse Lawyer's Manual*, he has served as legal counsel for Geronimo Pratt, the Republic of New Afrika, the New York 3, and other targets of political repression. He currently represents community groups in New York City.

RESOURCE ORGANIZATIONS

For educational materials and campaigns:

- Christic Institute, 1324 N. Capitol St. NW, Washington, DC 20002, (202) 797-8106
- Movement Support Network (an anti-repression project of the Center for Constitutional Rights in conjunction with the National Lawyers Guild), 666 Broadway, New York, NY 10012, (212) 614-6422
- National Alliance Against Racist and Political Repression 126 W. 119th St., New York, NY 10026, (212) 866-8600
- National Committee Against Repressive Legislation, 236 Massachusetts Ave. NE, #406, Washington, DC 20002, (202) 543-7659
- Political Rights Defense Fund, P.O. Box 649, Cooper Station, New York, NY 10003 (212) 691-3270

For legal advice and assistance:

- Center for Constitutional Rights, 666 Broadway, New York, NY 10012, (212) 614-6464
- Civil Liberties Union of Massachusetts, 19 Temple Pl., Boston, MA. 02111, (617) 482-3170
- Civil Liberties Union of Southern California, 663 S. Shatto Pl., Los Angeles, CA. 90005, (213) 487-1720 (Check to see if the civil liberties union in your area will help.)
- National Conference of Black Lawyers, 126 W. 119th St., New York, NY 10026, (212) 864-4000
- National Emergency Civil Liberties Committee, 175 Fifth Ave., New York, NY 10010, (212) 673-1360
- National Lawyers Guild, 55 Avenue of the Americas, New York, NY 10013, (212) 966-5000 or the NLG chapter near you.
- People's Law Office, 343 S. Dearborn, #1607, Chicago, IL. 60604, (312) 663-5046

For help with research and investigation:

- Anti-Repression Resource Team, P.O. Box 122, Jackson, MS 39205, (601) 969-2269
- Center for Investigative Reporting, Freedom of Information Project, 530 Howard, 2d Floor, San Francisco, CA. 94105, (415) 543-1200
- Data Center, 464 19th St., Oakland, CA. 94612, (415) 835-4692
- Fund for Open Information and Accountability, 145 W. Fourth St., New York, NY 10012, (212) 477-3188
- National Security Archives, 1755 Massachusetts Ave. N.W., #500, Washington, D.C. 20036, (202) 797-0882
- Political Research Associates, 678 Massachusetts Ave., #205, Cambridge, MA. 02139, (617) 661-9313